Editors: Catherine Bradley,
Don Slater
Art Director: Charles Matheson
Designers: Malcolm Smythe,
Richard Kay
Researcher: Cecilia Weston-Baker

Illustrated by Ron Hayward
Associates and Peter Bull

Designed and produced by
Aladdin Books Ltd
70 Old Compton Street
London W1V 5PA

© Aladdin Books Ltd 1986

First published in the
United States in 1987 by
Franklin Watts
387 Park Avenue South
New York NY 10016

ISBN 0 531 10322 6

Library of Congress Catalog
Card Number: 86 62903

Printed in Belgium

CONFLICT IN THE 20TH CENTURY

SOUTHEAST ASIA
FROM 1945

IAN BECKETT
Edited by Dr John Pimlott

FRANKLIN WATTS

New York · London · Toronto · Sydney

INTRODUCTION

The area known as Southeast Asia has been a source of conflict throughout the post-1945 period, reflecting many of the pressures and problems associated with the so-called "Developing World." A central theme is that of nationalism, for with the exception of Thailand and Brunei, all the countries of the area – present-day Burma, Malaysia, Singapore, Vietnam, Laos, Kampuchea, Indonesia and the Philippines – spent the immediate aftermath of the Second World War striving for independence from alien, mainly European, rule.

In some cases, notably those of Burma and the Philippines, this was achieved with relative ease, but elsewhere the process led to bitter, protracted struggles. These were often made more intense by the factor of communism, which elevated essentially regional conflicts to the level of the superpower divide. Nowhere was this more apparent than in Vietnam, where the United States fought a costly (and eventually fruitless) war to stem the tide of Marxist philosophy.

But this is only one aspect of the region's problems. Within many of the countries involved, the post-independence governments, whether democratic or otherwise, have not been accepted by all elements of a fragmented society. Minority groups, dedicated to the pursuit of rival political ideals or convinced that they have been excluded from a share in the running of the state because of racial or religious differences, have often been prepared to fight for their beliefs.

In some countries, such as Burma and the Philippines, this has led to periods of virtual civil war and chronic political instability. Elsewhere, such internal problems have been exploited by neighboring countries intent on territorial expansion, leading to border clashes or even outright war. The Vietnamese invasion of Kampuchea and clashes between Vietnamese and Thai forces show how easily trouble can spread.

The result is a region in which friction and hostility are commonplace, and although not all countries are equally affected – some, like Singapore and Brunei, are both peaceful and prosperous – the levels of violence have been, and continue to be, worryingly high.

DR JOHN PIMLOTT *Series Editor*

EDITORIAL PANEL

Series Editor:
Dr John Pimlott, Senior Lecturer in the Department of War Studies and International Affairs, RMA Sandhurst, UK

Editorial Advisory Panel:
Brigadier General James L Collins Jr, US Army Chief of Military History 1970-82

General Sir John Hackett, former Commander-in-Chief of the British Army of the Rhine and Principal of King's College, London, UK

Ian Hogg, retired Master Gunner of the Artillery, British Army, and editor of *Jane's Infantry Weapons*

John Keegan, former Senior Lecturer in the Department of War Studies and International Affairs, RMA Sandhurst, now Defense correspondent, *Daily Telegraph*

Professor Laurence Martin, Vice-Chancellor of the University of Newcastle-upon-Tyne, UK

The Author:
Dr Ian Beckett is a Senior Lecturer in the Department of War Studies and International Affairs, RMA Sandhurst, and a Fellow of the Royal Historical Society. He is the author of *Riflemen Form* and co-editor of *Politicians and Defence, Armed Forces and Modern Counter-Insurgency* and *A Nation in Arms*. He also contributed to *British Military Operations, 1945-84* and *Vietnam: The history and the tactics*.

The modern era brought years of mechanized war to the peasant societies of Southeast Asia. In Vietnam, an ox-cart clatters out of the way of US M48 medium tanks on an operation in search of Viet Cong guerrillas near Saigon, 1967.

CONTENTS

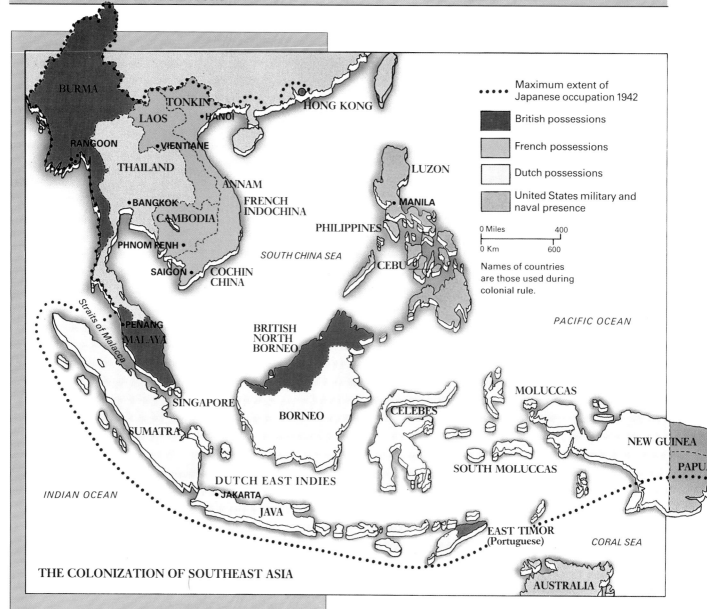

THE COLONIZATION OF SOUTHEAST ASIA

CHAPTER 1

AN AREA OF INSTABILITY

Southeast Asia is a vast region of great diversity. Of continuing strategic and economic importance to foreign powers, the area was dominated by colonial rule until the post-1945 era. The colonial system increased internal tensions but it also prompted a growing desire for national self-determination. However, it was the defeat of the colonial powers by the Japanese during the Second World War that raised the hopes of the people of the region for independence.

The enormous expanse of Southeast Asia embraces those countries which lie to the east of India, to the south of China and to the north of Australia: in other words, Burma, Thailand, Malaysia, Singapore, Vietnam, Laos, Kampuchea (Cambodia), Brunei, Indonesia and the Philippines. With Southeast Asia straddling the ocean routes between India and the Pacific, control over this area had major strategic importance for the Western colonial powers. Today it is still a focus of superpower interest both strategically and in terms of the increasing economic importance of the Pacific Basin in world trade and industry. Southeast Asia's global role contrasts with the underdeveloped nature of the region itself. It is made up of peoples of numerous races, religions and cultures, often combined into countries that sprawl across thousands of miles.

The sheer size of the region is difficult to grasp. In geographical terms, it is an extension of the continental landmass of Asia, where rugged mountains, cut by large swift-flowing rivers, jut out into the South China Sea and beyond, creating an immense archipelago, or group of islands, which extends for over 4,800 km (3,000 miles). Modern Indonesia embraces more than 13,000 separate islands and the Philippines over 7,000.

In many respects the rivers and seas of the region have shaped its economic and political development. The lower reaches of the great rivers have provided fertile plains, ideal for agriculture and settlements. Political boundaries have tended to follow the rivers. Within the archipelago, the same advantages have been provided by the seas around the islands, although some communities have become isolated.

Climate

The climate of Southeast Asia is tropical. The temperature is uniformly high throughout the year at sea level, although it decreases gradually where the ground rises to the mountains. Close to the Equator, which runs through the center of the region, heavy rain falls evenly during the year, but farther north the annual monsoons lead to a more disrupted pattern. The Northeast Monsoon, for example, brings heavy rainfall to the eastern continental states of Vietnam, Laos, Kampuchea (Cambodia), parts of Thailand and the Malay peninsula in the winter months, while the Southwest Monsoon inundates Burma and the western areas in the summer.

Tangled jungles are a principal feature of the terrain from Thailand to the south, although farther north and on the higher ground vegetation becomes more sparse. With the exception of the river plains and coastal fringes, the terrain is often extremely difficult to move through and village settlements are isolated.

In the village areas, agriculture can be quite primitive, based upon the principle of "slash and burn," whereby small areas of jungle are cleared by fire and crops grown until the land is exhausted. This often compares dramatically with the rich ricefields of the river plains, where the mud deposited by the annual monsoon-floods contains plenty of nutrients.

Economic activity

The region contains few natural resources that can be easily exploited. In mineral terms, there are deposits of tin in the Malay peninsula and southern Thailand, coal in northern Vietnam and some gold in the Philippines, but it was not until the discovery of oil in Burma, Brunei and Indonesia that economic growth began.

Elsewhere, agriculture has remained a key source of wealth, and this can vary from country to country, according to the traditions of colonial rule in many cases. Indeed, colonization overturned the traditional subsistence farming (producing just enough to live on) and substituted "cash crops" which may be sold for a profit. The exploitation of such crops as rubber, oil palm, sugar, copra, coffee and tobacco has taken place in the last 100 years, introducing the region to the processes of international trade.

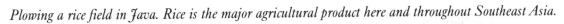

Plowing a rice field in Java. Rice is the major agricultural product here and throughout Southeast Asia.

This has created only limited wealth, in the absence of industrial development on a large scale, with countries such as Laos, Kampuchea, Burma, Vietnam and Indonesia all being among those with the lowest *per capita* income – the average amount earned in a year by one person – in the modern world.

This does not mean that the region is unimportant in economic terms, for it has always been a center for trade, acting as a market place for the goods of Asia and attracting interest from countries elsewhere, particularly Europe. This has led to the development of major ports such as Singapore, Penang, Bangkok, Manila and Jakarta, where wealth can be generated and economic strength built up. Singapore, for example, is currently one of the richest countries in the Far East, even though it contains no natural resources and hardly any agriculture.

Social problems

Divisions between rich and poor have undoubtedly contributed to the tensions of Southeast Asia, leading to a shift of population away from the poverty-stricken rural areas into the cities, where apparent wealth and Western-style sophistication act as a powerful magnet. Unfortunately, the cities often cannot absorb large numbers of unskilled people, and this can result in unrest, as the newcomers face a lack of jobs, housing and social services. The population of the region has grown at an alarming rate, helped in part by improved medical facilities.

Inevitably, in a region covering some five million square kilometers (two million square miles) of land area, different groups of people have emerged. Successive waves of peoples from the heart of Asia have moved into the region over the centuries, putting pressure on earlier migrants and driving them into remote mountain areas or to isolated islands.

As a result, most countries in Southeast Asia have ethnic minorities – groups of people sharing a common language or culture – scattered far from the main centers of population. Examples are the Karen, Kachin and Mon hill-tribes of Burma, the Dyaks of Borneo and the Moi (known to the French as *Montagnard*) peoples of Vietnam. Frequently, such people have been difficult to absorb into the newly-created countries of the 20th century and have acted as sources of trouble.

Social divisions: a "floating community" versus high-rise living

Managing ethnic diversity: A Burmese tribal family about to be moved to a resettlement camp.

Racial problems

Racial tensions have also been heightened by the often ill-defined borders of the countries that emerged from the European period of rule. The colonial powers often left the borders vague or imposed boundaries which bore little relation to tribal or ethnic realities.

In French Indochina (now Vietnam, Laos and Kampuchea) this was particularly the case. Many Vietnamese, for example, found themselves living in what became Kampuchea, while many Khmers (the people of Kampuchea) ended up in Thailand, where they joined others who looked to Malaya as their natural homeland. This has led to border disputes and attempts by one country to annex (take over) the areas containing "their" people. This happened as recently as 1978, when the Vietnamese invaded Kampuchea and installed a new government.

Of equal significance has been the large number of Chinese in the region, who were attracted by the commercial opportunities created by the European powers. They have often acted as a focus for violence by local people resentful of their apparent wealth.

For example, the Chinese account for over 75 per cent of the population of modern Singapore and there has been trouble between them and the comparatively small number of remaining Malays. Indeed, the decision by Singapore to leave the Malaysian Federation in 1965 was partly a result of these racial problems. The Chinese did not want to be absorbed into a new political arrangement in which they would suddenly become the minority.

Colonization by Europe

In terms of understanding the development of Southeast Asia in the 20th century, the impact of the Europeans cannot be overestimated. Over the centuries, European countries gradually infiltrated the region, initially in search of the fabled "spice islands." The first to arrive were the Portuguese, who seized the Malay peninsula in 1511. The Portuguese were challenged by the Spanish, who moved into the Philippines taking Cebu in 1565 and Luzon six years later, and then by the Dutch, who created a settlement on the Malay coast at Malacca in 1641.

In turn, the Dutch came under pressure from British commercial interests. Although the latter tended to concentrate on India, they spread into Southeast Asia as Dutch financial strength declined in the 18th century. The British were granted land in Penang in 1791 and at Singapore in 1819, while Burma was annexed between 1824 and 1886. As the British developed a firm hold on the Malay peninsula and moved eastwards into parts of Borneo, they gradually gained a strong strategic grip on key areas.

Between 1859 and 1899, France extended its control over Laos, Cambodia and the territories of modern Vietnam. The last colonial power to arrive was the United States, which occupied the Philippines after defeating the Spanish in 1898.

Thus, by the beginning of the 20th century, a pattern of Western occupation had emerged, reflecting the strategic and economic priorities of outside powers. To the British, control of Burma was essential to protect the approaches to India from the east, while settlements in Malaya, Singapore and parts of Borneo ensured free passage for British ships through the Straits of Malacca – one of the few routes linking the Indian and Pacific Oceans – with the potential of denying similar passage to enemies in wartime. Chief among these "enemies" was France, firmly established in Indochina. The fact that Thailand remained the only unoccupied country reflected its value as a "buffer," preventing Anglo-French clashes that might have led to a more general war.

Dutch occupation of the East Indies, surviving Portuguese interests in East Timor and, most recently of all, United States influence in the Philippines merely increased the chances of conflict between the occupying powers, all of which were finding that, strategic considerations apart, the areas under their authority were important in economic terms. Most would not give them up lightly.

Colonial rule

The nature of colonial rule varied from area to area – in British colonies, for example, government authority extended down to village level, whereas to the French, Dutch and Americans, the key was control of the major towns, ports and markets. But one thing was clear: colonial rule existed for the benefit of the colonial ruler. Advantages may have emerged in terms of improved medical, social and educational facilities, and a measure of imposed political stability, but these were invariably the by-products of colonial systems based upon policies of exploitation, designed solely to enrich the colonial rulers.

The colonial system completely transformed the region. The extraction of minerals and the new methods of agriculture introduced by outside countries destroyed traditional economic structures in many areas. This threatened local cultures, particularly when, as part of European rule, new religions and educational methods were also introduced. In the process, local inhabitants often lost control of their land and their livelihoods were threatened by the Asian immigrants brought in to provide cheap labor or to set up new businesses.

Ho Chi Minh, leader of the Vietnamese communists

The growth of nationalism

These problems took time to emerge, particularly as the European powers reacted forcibly to any signs of opposition. Between 1930 and 1932, for example, the Saya San uprising in Burma, triggered by economic resentment among the local people, was put down by British-controlled armed forces. The Americans responded in a similar way in the Philippines in 1935 when faced by the Sakdal peasant revolt.

However, by that time, more general opposition had begun to emerge in parts of Southeast Asia, as subject peoples slowly awoke to the idea of nationalism, demanding the right to govern themselves. In many cases, this was a natural by-product of Western education, which stressed the principles of freedom and self-determination while denying them to colonial populations, and some of the nationalist leaders who emerged were first introduced to the new ideas through the colonial system.

The early Indonesian nationalist, Mohammad Hatta, for example, spent 10 years as an economics student in the Netherlands before returning to the Dutch East Indies (as Indonesia was then known) in 1932 to work for independence. Many leaders spent years in exile in the West.

The spread of communism

The impact of communism was even more significant. Stressing such aims as common ownership of land and its products, communism found a ready source of support among the oppressed peoples of colonial areas, particularly when it promised to overthrow the colonial system and achieve the desires of nationalism. The Russian model, based upon the actions of urban industrial workers, may have proved inapplicable to agricultural Southeast Asia – it was to take the peasant theories of the Chinese communist leader Mao Tse-tung to produce a workable alternative – but the basic principles were influential from the 1920s.

For example, Nguyen Ai Quoc, better known as Ho Chi Minh, left his native Vietnam in 1911 as a member of a ship's crew bound for Europe. Arriving in Paris in 1917, he became familiar with the ideas of socialism and was actually one of the founders of the French Communist Party in 1920. Returning to Vietnam, he led the Revolutionary League of the Youth of Vietnam which, in turn, produced the Indochinese Communist Party in 1929. By then, communist parties had also emerged in Malaya, Burma, the Dutch East Indies and the Philippines, creating an underground political opposition to the continuance of Western rule.

Growing opposition to colonial rule

There were also other influences. Indonesian nationalism drew much of its spiritual support from Islam, and Buddhism was equally important in the development of Burmese demands for independence. Generally, too, colonial rule helped to unify areas physically by establishing ports, towns, railways and roads, bringing people together in ways that would have been impossible a few years earlier.

The result was a steady rise in the number and strength of opposition groups in the 1920s and 1930s, some of which were suppressed quite ruthlessly by the colonial authorities. In 1930, for example, risings by the Vietnamese Nationalist Party and the communists – the "Ngeh-Tinh Soviets" – failed disastrously in the face of determined French response.

Such pressures were not universal throughout Southeast Asia at this time: in some areas the people appeared content with existing arrangements. The United States' commitment to Philippine independence reduced tensions there, while the Laotian and Khmer people showed little desire for self-determination, lacking the unifying structure of strong communist or nationalist political parties. What was needed was a powerful agent of change to persuade the people of Southeast Asia as a whole that colonial rule could be overthrown and replaced – and that was provided in late 1941 with the sudden attack on the Western colonies by Japan.

Japanese expansion

For Southeast Asia, the serious fighting began with Japan's spectacular run of victories against the European powers and the United States from December 1941 to May 1942, exposing them to humiliating defeat and effectively expelling them from the region. Japan's entry into the war was a gamble to secure a strong position (and, above all, the oilfields of the Dutch East Indies). Japan then hoped to achieve a lasting peace, avoiding furthur wars with the allied powers.

In the event, the surprise attack on the US Pacific Fleet at Pearl Harbor on December 7, 1941, coupled with the fact that the other colonial powers were fighting for survival in Europe or had already been occupied by the Germans, allowed the Japanese to enjoy remarkable military success in Southeast Asia. American outposts at Guam and Wake Island in the Pacific were overwhelmed, British forces in Hong Kong were defeated and a series of landings were made throughout the Western colonial areas.

The Malay peninsula and Singapore fell to the Japanese by February 15, 1942, after one of the most disastrous military campaigns in British history; Dutch naval resources were overwhelmed in the Battle of the Java Sea on February 27 and the Dutch East Indies surrendered on March 9. The last American bastion in the Philippines – the fortress of Corregidor – fell on May 6 and, by the end of that month, the British were in full retreat in Burma. By then both Thailand and French Indochina were under Japanese influence.

In the space of six months the Japanese had created a "Greater East Asia Coprosperity Sphere," embracing over 90 million people. So-called "victory disease" tempted the Japanese to extend their objectives until checked by the American naval victories at the battles of Coral Sea, May 7/8, and Midway June 4, 1942.

Japanese rule

The impact of these Japanese victories cannot be emphasized too highly. In particular, the surrender of 130,000 Allied troops at Singapore and the spectacle of American soldiers marching into captivity in the Philippines dealt a shattering blow to the prestige of colonial powers throughout Asia, exploding the myth that they were invincible. This undoubtedly boosted the anticolonial movements in the region, and would make it difficult for the colonial powers to reestablish their control.

To begin with, in 1941-42, the Japanese seemed to offer nationalist groups the opportunity for independence, even if it was on their terms and geared towards creating a solidly anti-Western territorial bloc in Southeast Asia. In Burma, for example, the Japanese sponsored a Burma Independence (later National) Army in December 1941 under the command of Aung San, and on August 1, 1943, the country was granted limited and formal "independence" under the leadership of a former prime minister, Dr. U Ba Maw. A similar degree of "independence" was granted to the Philippines in 1943, and if the Japanese had not been defeated in August 1945, they would probably have completed their creation of KRIS, a movement aimed at promoting union between Indonesia and Malaya.

But it soon became obvious that such plans and policies were not in the best interests of the local people. Japanese rule began to reveal a ruthless determination to extract as much as possible in economic terms from the occupied countries. It became apparent that the events of 1941-42 had merely substituted one form of colonialism for another.

Short-lived as it was, the Japanese empire in the Pacific and Southeast Asia both inspired and oppressed the people within it. Japanese expansion was well documented both for home consumption and propoganda purposes. Below, a staged photograph taken in 1942 shows Japanese officers beneath their flag, surveying a recent acquisition – an island in the Philippines.

The growth of nationalist groups

Nationalist groups, however, could use the Japanese policy of "independence" to gain political ground or as a focus for popular opposition. In Indonesia, for example, the Japanese initially allowed nationalists such as Hatta and Kusno Sukarno to establish the *Putera* (Center of Power) organization in March 1943, but when this quickly developed into a purely nationalist rather than a pro-Japanese party, they were forced to disband it in 1944.

Even when, right at the end of the war, the Japanese promised immediate independence to the Indonesians, they had to make the offer to Hatta and Sukarno, by now enjoying a considerable degree of popular support. Indeed, the Indonesian leaders took the opportunity to declare their own independence on August 17, 1945, defying both the defeated Japanese and the Dutch – the latter of whom were intent on regaining control once the war was over.

Indochina was different in that Bao Dai – the emperor who collaborated with the Japanese and finally took complete control of the area in March 1945 – did not represent any political party or organization which enjoyed popular support. The nationalists, who had popular backing, spent the period after 1941 building up armed opposition ("resistance") to Japanese rule. In this they were helped by the Allies, particularly the American Office of Strategic Services (OSS).

In the Philippines, nationalist guerrillas were even incorporated into the United States Armed Forces in the Far East (USAFFE), receiving training, arms and other supplies on a regular basis. Elsewhere in the Philippines, however, the resistance groups were associated with prewar peasant unions and, significantly, the communists, many of whom already had underground bases and arms dumps from the period of anticolonial activity in the 1920s and 1930s. On March 29, 1942, these clandestine groups met together to form the *Hukbo ng Bayan lagan sa Hapon* (People's Anti-Japanese Army), known in an abbreviated form as the *Hukbalahap*, or *Huks*. They were to be a major source of trouble to the postwar government.

A similar pattern emerged in Malaya, where the British Force 136 sponsored resistance groups. However, during most of the Occupation it was the communist Malayan People's Anti-Japanese Army (MPAJA) that carried out guerrilla raids on the occupying troops. Finally, in Indochina, it was the communists who led the way, forming the *Viet Nam Doc Lap Dong Minh Hoi* (League for the Independence of Vietnam, usually shortened to *Viet Minh*) in May 1941, led by Ho Chi Minh. They received support from the OSS in the final months of the war, although they seemed to spend much of their time building up political support among the people rather than mounting major attacks on the enemy.

The end of Japanese rule

By 1945, therefore, groups such as the *Viet Minh* and MPAJA were well placed to make the most of the Japanese surrender. In Indochina, Ho Chi Minh took the opportunity to declare an independent Democratic Republic of Vietnam in Hanoi, the capital of Tonkin, on September 2, 1945. He was aided in this by OSS officers which implied that he had American support. The rulers of Laos and Cambodia followed suit.

In Malaya, where a return of British troops was only to be expected (chiefly because, unlike the French, the British did have soldiers in the Far East), the MPAJA enjoyed three weeks between the Japanese surrender and the arrival of their "liberators" in which to establish their popularity and to seize Japanese arms. Even in Burma, where Aung San effectively changed sides as soon as the Japanese began to lose the war, his newly-formed Anti-Fascist People's Freedom League (AFPFL) made significant political gains, although in this case the country was liberated by Allied forces, who recaptured the capital Rangoon in May 1945.

The Second World War was thus a "watershed" in the history of Southeast Asia. In four years not only had the colonial rulers been discredited in the eyes of the local people, but the experience of Japanese occupation had either created or reinforced demands for future independence. In many countries, this had led to the growth of strong nationalist movements, some of which were also communist, and it seemed unlikely that the prewar colonial powers would be either willing or able to reassert their presence.

The latter point was apparently underlined by the Western Allies' wartime emphasis upon political "freedom" and by the actions of the United States in encouraging decolonization. Unfortunately, the Europeans had other ideas. As the British, French and Dutch returned, intent on regaining control as if nothing had happened, the nationalists prepared to use force to achieve their stated aims. In the process, all the underlying ethnic, religious and territorial tensions of the region came to the surface, making the immediate postwar period one in which violence and instability were inevitable.

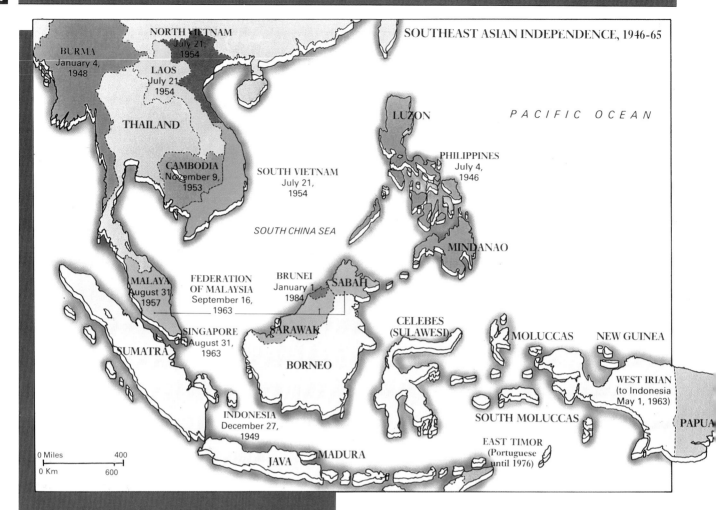

SOUTHEAST ASIAN INDEPENDENCE, 1946-65

CHAPTER 2

THE STRUGGLE FOR INDEPENDENCE, 1945-1965

In the 20-year period after 1945, colonial rule was dismantled throughout Southeast Asia. In most cases, the process involved violence, with nationalists pitted against either the European powers or the Western-syle governments they installed. The nationalists pursued a new form of armed struggle: revolutionary warfare, often modeled on Mao Tse-tung's strategy in China. Taken by surprise at first, the colonial powers developed techniques of "counterinsurgency" to meet the threat.

When the Japanese announced their surrender on August 15, 1945, a peaceful transfer of power to local nationalists in Southeast Asia was widely expected, given the four-year interruption in Western colonial rule. Vast areas of previously European possessions were still under Japanese control, despite the liberation of Burma and most of the Philippines. Plans for Allied landings in Malaya and the Dutch East Indies were not far enough advanced to be carried out straight away, and neither the French nor the Dutch had forces in the Far East in 1945.

The Allies had decided earlier in 1945 that forces would be sent to the occupied areas to ensure that Japanese troops in the region were disarmed and sent home. Thus, the British would go into the Dutch East Indies and southern Indochina, while Nationalist Chinese *(Kuomintang)* units would enter northern Vietnam. They were not ordered specifically to prepare the way for a return of Dutch or French rulers, but the fact that they would be on the spot with superior forces to those of the nationalists inevitably created an opportunity for such a return to take place.

Guerrilla warfare

The nationalists therefore found that they would have to fight to prevent a return to colonialism, and in this they had a number of advantages. Their involvement in the struggle against the Japanese gave them some popular support and combat experience. Having declared independence in the period between the Japanese surrender and the arrival of the Allied forces, the nationalists were able to set up governments which were, in many cases, acceptable to the people.

More significantly, their experience of resistance had revealed the effectiveness of guerrilla warfare, in which lightly armed fighters, enjoying local support and knowledge of terrain, harass and wear down a militarily superior enemy.

The Chinese communist leader Mao Tse-tung had written about such warfare as early as 1938, and although there is no evidence that all postwar nationalists were fully aware of his teachings, a significant number, including Ho Chi Minh in Vietnam and Chin Peng, the MPAJA commander in Malaya, were clearly influenced by his example. When Mao succeeded in gaining power in Peking in October 1949, defeating the *Kuomintang* armies under Chiang Kai-shek, his influence was assured.

Even in those areas where communism was not the driving force behind the nationalists, guerrilla warfare emerged and a Maoist-style revolution was attempted. The basic form of such a revolution, therefore, colored much of the history of Southeast Asia during the postwar period.

Members of the Chinese People's Liberation Army.

Mao's revolution relied on the ordinary people.

Mao Tse-tung's ideas

Mao's basic aim was to gain political power and he recognized very early on in his career that the main instruments at his disposal were the ordinary peasants who, by sheer weight of numbers, could overwhelm the existing government. But the people had to be organized and persuaded to support the revolution, and here, in Mao's case, the structure of the Communist Party was crucial.

If small "cadres" or groups of communists could be organized in remote rural areas, out of reach of the security forces of the existing government, secure bases of revolutionary support would be established. These would contain people who were dedicated to opposing colonial or repressive regimes, and would be protected by the people themselves, organized into guerrilla groups. They could then extend their area of control by attacking isolated government outposts, ambushing security force patrols and generally harassing the enemy, most of whom would be fighting in rural areas they did not know and with no popular support.

Meanwhile, other secure bases would be established elsewhere, creating a situation which has been likened to ink spots on blotting paper: gradually the paper will be covered in ink, spreading naturally as it is absorbed. Eventually, the guerrillas will be stronger than the demoralized and spread-out security forces, upon which they can emerge as a full-scale army and defeat their enemy in open battle. This will expose the existing government to political defeat, enabling the revolutionaries to assume power. Admittedly, this was the "ideal" and it did not always work precisely in the way proposed by Mao, but it was a sufficiently new form of warfare to take the colonial powers by surprise.

The communist coup in Vietnam

The Maoist style of warfare first emerged in Indochina, where Ho Chi Minh had declared independence on September 2, 1945. His new government, based upon the political and military organization of the *Viet Minh*, was stronger in the north (Tonkin and parts of Annam) than it was in the south (Cochin China and southern Annam), and when the British committed forces to Saigon, the capital of Cochin China, on September 11, he soon found his control slipping in that area.

British troops, commanded by Major-General Douglas Gracey, released the French forces imprisoned by the Japanese and even went so far as to rearm Japanese Marines in an attempt to restore order. When French reinforcements arrived in May 1946, they were able to resume control up to the line of the 16th parallel. North of that line, the *Kuomintang* had marched in to disarm and repatriate the Japanese, according to the Allied agreement, but they did not interfere with the communist government in Hanoi. By mid-1946, the southern part of Vietnam, plus Cambodia and Laos, had been returned to French rule, leaving the northern part isolated and vulnerable to French attack.

The French response

But for some time the French, wary about entering a war so soon after the Second World War, tried to negotiate with Ho Chi Minh, who was willing to talk so long as there was a chance of gaining political recognition for his new regime.

The French were prepared to offer limited self-government to Vietnam, under the nominal leadership of the Emperor Bao Dai. However, the restrictions imposed on nationalist freedom and the lack of trust enjoyed by Bao Dai – he had, after all, accepted a similar position of "leadership' from the Japanese – soon caused the negotiations to break down.

In November 1946, French forces attacked *Viet Minh* positions in Tonkin and soon regained control of Hanoi. What they did not realize was that Ho Chi Minh, acting on the advice of his brilliant military commander, Vo Nguyen Giap, had already withdrawn his best fighting men to remote bases in the northeast (the Viet Bac) and to the difficult terrain of the Red River delta. Both were areas of strong political support for the *Viet Minh*, following the Maoist idea that secure bases were the key to survival and eventual victory.

To the French, the ease with which they had reentered Hanoi and then set up small garrisons throughout the northern provinces suggested that the *Viet Minh* had been defeated. For the next three years they acted defensively, little realizing that this was just what Ho Chi Minh required. As he concentrated on consolidating his support among the peasants in remote rural areas and building up his guerrilla forces, the French resumed their prewar colonial policies as if nothing had changed.

The French set up defensive lines as well as outposts to dominate local areas, but they failed to mount offensive operations. *Viet Minh* attacks in 1950 took them completely by surprise and, as the outposts fell to locally superior guerrilla bands, a bitter campaign began. It was to continue for the next four years.

The First Indochina War

The French, having experienced nothing like this before, treated the war as a normal conflict between rival armed forces, failing to appreciate that Ho Chi Minh's main aim was to prepare the way for a political revolution. As a result, most of the French Expeditionary Force, which included Vietnamese units, were ordered to defend a series of fortifications around Hanoi known as the De Lattre Line.

Very few units were left for attacks on *Viet Minh* territory. Some were mounted, but the use of troops who were neither trained nor prepared to fight in remote jungle areas played into the hands of the guerrillas. In 1951, *Viet Minh* units were caught in the open and badly mauled by French forces with artillery and aircraft, but this was unusual.

During Operation Lorraine in late 1952, for example, a huge French force left the safety of the De Lattre Line to capture enemy supply dumps along the banks of the Clear River, and although they succeeded in reaching their objectives, they failed to engage *Viet Minh* units and were soon forced to withdraw as their lines of supply became stretched. As soon as this move began, with French forces strung out along single-lane tracks, the guerrillas struck. By the time the French had reached the De Lattre Line, nearly 1,200 of their soldiers had been killed, often without having seen an enemy fighter.

Such attacks were demoralizing and, as the casualties mounted, increasingly unpopular, especially among the people in France itself, who had no idea of the unique nature of the war. In addition, once the communists had gained power in China, the *Viet Minh* had been guaranteed support that the French could never hope to match.

THE FIRST INDOCHINA WAR

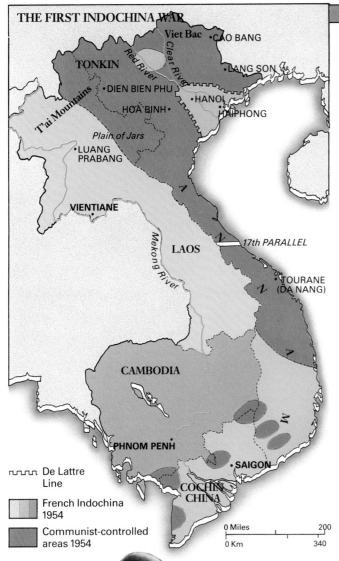

De Lattre Line

French Indochina 1954

Communist-controlled areas 1954

0 Miles — 200
0 Km — 340

Moreover, supplies were distributed to the guerrillas by thousands of porters drawn from the peasant revolutionaries. By 1953, with the French bottled up around Hanoi and on the Plain of Jars in Laos, in response to *Viet Minh* attacks, another communist victory seemed likely.

The French defeat at Dien Bien Phu

But the French still had superior firepower and, if the *Viet Minh* could be tempted to come out into open battle, it was felt that they could still be defeated. For this reason, the French decided to mount an airborne assault on the village of Dien Bien Phu, in the northwest of Tonkin, in November 1953, threatening *Viet Minh* supply lines into Laos and forcing them to respond on ground of French choosing. Situated in the center of a heart-shaped valley some 274 km (170 miles) from Hanoi, Dien Bien Phu was quickly transformed into a fortified camp, resupplied by air, and the French confidently waited to be attacked, presuming that the enemy would be unable to bring heavy weapons through the surrounding jungle.

Left: Vietnamese soldiers with the French expeditionary force fighting the Viet Minh, *January 1954.*
Below: French paratroops defending a perimeter trench at Dien Bien Phu.

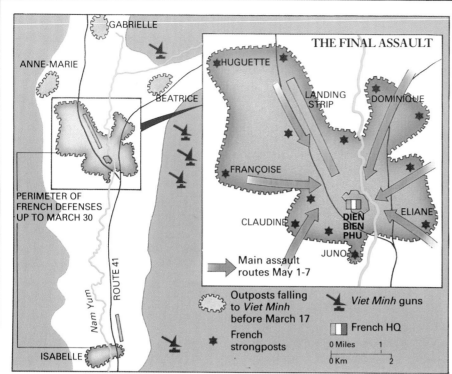

THE FINAL ASSAULT

GABRIELLE

ANNE-MARIE

BEATRICE

HUGUETTE

LANDING STRIP

DOMINIQUE

FRANÇOISE

PERIMETER OF FRENCH DEFENSES UP TO MARCH 30

CLAUDINE

DIEN BIEN PHU

ELIANE

JUNO

Main assault routes May 1-7

Outposts falling to *Viet Minh* before March 17

French strongposts

Viet Minh guns

French HQ

0 Miles 1
0 Km 2

ISABELLE

ROUTE 41

Nam Yum

Dien Bien Phu
November 20, 1953-May 7, 1954.
The French aim at Dien Bien Phu was to create a fortified position which would tempt the Viet Minh *into an open battle they could not win. In reality, the situation was reversed.* Viet Minh *forces, holding the high ground, used artillery to close the airstrips and took out the isolated northern outposts (Anne-Marie, Gabrielle and Beatrice) before laying close siege to the main French positions. The French defenders were gradually worn down and pushed back until, in early May, cut off, outmaneuvered and outfought, they were forced to surrender and march into captivity.*

Unfortunately, they had reckoned without the ingenuity and political dedication of the ordinary people, many of whom flocked willingly to the area to construct a supply route along which antiaircraft guns, supplied by the Chinese, could be dragged. Once these were in position on hills overlooking the French base, the air link with Hanoi was threatened and the garrison was suddenly left vulnerable.

Viet Minh attacks, backed by ordinary artillery pieces, gradually closed the ring around Dien Bien Phu, and although the French forces fought bravely, they could not hold out indefinitely, particularly when the annual monsoon flooded many of their positions on the valley floor. After a 55-day siege, the last of the defenders surrendered on May 7, 1954. Over 9,000 French troops marched into captivity, symbols of a defeat from which the colonial rulers in Hanoi could not recover.

The communist victory in North Vietnam

The communists used their military success to achieve political victory, exploiting the demoralization of the French and the unpopularity of the war in France itself to bring about a favorable peace settlement. Negotiations began in Geneva without delay and, on July 21, 1954, the French agreed to withdraw from Indochina. The independence granted to Laos and Cambodia was to be recognized and Vietnam was to be divided along

the line of the 17th parallel. To the north, Ho Chi Minh was to be left to govern the Democratic Republic of North Vietnam; to the south, a new, more Western-orientated Republic of South Vietnam was to be established, covering areas which had been less affected by the spread of communism. It was the first of the nationalist victories, but was, in communist eyes, still incomplete: until the whole of Indochina had fallen to their rule, the war would go on. The world had not heard the last of Vietnam.

Communist victory undoubtedly owed much to the French failure to appreciate the new style of warfare. Coupled to Mao's own victory in China, it began to seem that such an approach was unstoppable, particularly as similar campaigns were being fought by communists elsewhere in Southeast Asia.

But this was not necessarily the case, for government forces in both Malaya and the Philippines were turning the tide, evolving tactics and techniques known as "counterinsurgency" to combat revolutionary tactics. In neither country were the communists as well organized or popular as the *Viet Minh* in northern Vietnam, and both the British and the Filipinos were able to learn from the French defeat. They worked on preparing more successful countermoves, and the fact that they prevented a further spread of communism was crucial to the future of Southeast Asia as a whole.

Communist pressure in Malaya

In Malaya, the impact of Maoism was restricted to the Chinese population. Brought into the colony by the British as laborers and traders, the Chinese had retained a separate identity and culture. Although only a small minority were affected by the spread of Maoist ideas, their activities clearly constituted a threat, particularly to those Malayan nationalists who were working for independence from British rule. The latter wanted a separate Malayan state, not a communist "puppet" ruled from Peking.

The Malayan communists were actually ill-prepared for the kind of protracted struggle demanded by Maoist theory. The MPAJA had never been truly tested in battle against the Japanese during the Second World War and had been disbanded in December 1945 in return for the legal recognition of the Malayan Communist Party (MCP) by the returning British. Although strong among trade unions, the MCP made little political headway because of its dependence upon the minority Chinese population for its support.

This gave it little influence among the vast majority of the Malay population as was seen when the emerging United Malayan National Organization, a Malay movement, successfully challenged British plans for a Malay Union in which the Chinese would have enjoyed some representation. Instead the British were forced to propose a federation – a form of central government in which the different states or provinces of a country retain some control over their own affairs – with far more restricted rights for the Chinese. Once this had been announced in 1948, the only hope of communist victory lay in a Maoist-style revolution.

As in Indochina, the intention of the communists was to establish secure bases in the jungle from which to mount attacks on the police, government officials and economic structure of the country, wearing down the resolve of the British to persist with their federation plans. Unfortunately, the Malayan Races Liberation Army (MRLA), as the MCP called its forces, was not fully prepared. A number of arms dumps had been established in 1945, but all other supplies had to come from Chinese "squatters." These were people who had been forced to leave their homes through the closure of mines and estates by the Japanese and had settled on undeveloped land on the fringes of the jungle, to which they had no legal title.

For the majority of the Malay population, enjoying a reasonably prosperous standard of living and secure in the belief that the British would indeed grant the independence promised, the MRLA had little appeal, but to the Chinese squatters the future looked bleak and the political promise of the communists seemed worth fighting to achieve.

Peasants supply the Viet Minh *at Dien Bien Phu by bicycle.*

The British response

The MRLA campaign of guerrilla attacks began with some success, exploiting a lack of coordination between the police, the army and the civil authorities in Malaya. But the British declared a "State of Emergency" on June 17, 1948, and introduced a series of measures designed to ensure government control. Emergency laws were passed which allowed imprisonment of suspects without trial, the death penalty for anyone arrested carrying arms or explosives and the issue of special passes to everyone over the age of 12.

This was the beginning of one of the most successful counterinsurgency campaigns of the post-1945 period, based firmly upon the British realization that the aim of the insurgents was to gain political power, using the support of local people to overthrow existing colonial rule. Unlike the French in Indochina, who saw the problem as essentially military and responded accordingly, the British in Malaya concentrated on discovering who was the enemy and how he was organized before introducing policies designed to persuade the people to support the existing government and to isolate the insurgents. This prepared the way for selective military action against the guerrillas. It was a model that was to prove remarkably successful in Malaya and one that could be used elsewhere.

In Malaya, the process began in 1950, when Lieutenant-General Sir Harold Briggs drew up the "Briggs' Plan," which coordinated military and intelligence efforts at all levels and initiated an all-out effort to smash the guerrillas' political organization, the so-called *Min Yuen.* The squatters were then resettled in over 400 "New Villages," containing medical and educational facilities as well as permanent buildings and running water. Once these had been set up, far from the areas of guerrilla activity, and the squatters had been given many of the advantages they had lacked before, the guerrillas became isolated.

Despite these measures, however, the MRLA managed to carry out some remarkably effective attacks, including the assassination of the British High Commissioner, Sir Henry Gurney, on October 6, 1951. His successor, Sir Gerald Templer, promised early elections leading to independence and placed considerable emphasis on winning the "hearts and minds" of the ordinary people, convincing them that the government was worth supporting and that the guerrillas were the enemies of freedom.

Captured Malayan communists, 1948. Moments later all were killed by guerrilla snipers – as a security precaution.

This was so successful that whole sectors of the population actively aided the security forces, providing intelligence and reporting the presence of MRLA activists. The separation of the guerrilla from the people was achieved, forcing the MRLA to seek refuge in the jungles, far from the centers of population.

But the British would not let them rest, using their security forces to pursue the guerrillas and destroy their base camps. Specialist jungle fighters such as the Special Air Service (SAS) Regiment parachuted into the jungle to gain information and mount ambushes, while ordinary infantry soldiers patrolled guerrilla-affected areas, trapping the MRLA survivors. The guerrillas, far from enjoying the advantages of surprise and local support, as Mao presumed, suddenly found the situation reversed.

The defeat of the Malayan communists

By 1954, the MRLA was already a broken force. Moreover, an Alliance Party had been created, which included the United Malayan National Organization and other groups representing both the Chinese and Indian minorities.

Thus, when independence was granted on August 31, 1957, Malaya was able to develop free from the pressure of communism. The government rejected an offer by the communist leader Chin Peng to lay down arms in exchange for legal recognition of the MCP. However, it announced an amnesty, in which remaining guerrillas could surrender without having to face trial. By July 1960, some 6,000 guerrillas had been killed, 1,200 captured and 2,700 had surrendered since the beginning of the Emergency. The remnants of the MRLA withdrew across the border into southern Thailand, carrying out occasional guerrilla attacks for some time, but they no longer posed a real threat. The Maoist model had clearly failed in Malaya.

The new government could not ignore the problems associated with the ethnic divide, and since 1960 sustained efforts have been made to integrate the Chinese and Malay populations. These have not always enjoyed success, being based upon an insistence that the Chinese adopt the Malay language and abandon cultural separatism – a rather one-sided arrangement that led to widespread riots and a suspension of parliamentary democracy in the late 1960s. The ethnic question still threatens the future of the state, despite the creation of the Malaysian Federation in 1963.

British troops on patrol, Malaya, 1957.

The Philippines

In the Philippines, the communists had the advantage of being able to exploit genuine peasant grievances in the provinces of the island of Luzon. Population growth and a policy of dividing up the land into ever smaller packages to satisfy demand had left many peasants deeply in debt to their landlords. When the latter returned after the Japanese surrender in 1945, their demands for money, coupled with a fall in agricultural prices, lower wages and growing unemployment, led to widespread discontent and the formation of a National Peasants' Union (PKM) under the leadership of former *Huks*.

The PKM then joined with other groups, including the communists, in a Democratic Alliance (DA) to contest the April 1946 elections. The DA won all the seats in Central Luzon but the government debarred them in May on the grounds of alleged electoral fraud. Negotiations broke down and the *Huks*, now formally known as the *Hukbong Mapagpalaya ng Batan* (People's Liberation Army), took to the hills led by the wartime commander of the *Hukbalahap*, Luis Taruc.

It was never a purely communist uprising and the peasants had far more limited aims than the communist leadership (with whom Taruc eventually broke), but many of the characteristics of a Maoist-style insurgency were apparent. The rebels withdrew to secure base camps and mounted a series of hit-and-run attacks on government positions.

In this they were helped initially by the disastrous response of the government – created on July 4, 1946, as a direct copy of that of the United States – for although the *Huk* cause had little popular support outside Luzon, the government of Manuel Roxas resorted to a "mailed fist" policy which alienated the population. As police and army units swept into action after September 1946, treating all civilians as suspect and using excessive violence in their search for rebel bases, the *Huks* became accepted by many as the protectors of the people against the repressive central authorities. The government was also clearly incapable of recognizing the need for land reform or for political moves designed to undermine the popularity of the rebel groups.

The defeat of the Huks

Roxas' successor, Elpidio Quirino, attempted negotiations in June 1948, but these broke down in August and *Huk* successes continued. However, in September 1950 he appointed a former USAFFE guerrilla leader,

Ramon Magsaysay, as Secretary for National Defense. Magsaysay launched a "hearts and minds" program to win over the population to the government side. The despised police force was integrated with the army, given better pay to discourage looting and barred from using excessive force. An economic Development Corps, staffed by Army engineers, was set up to bring roads, schools, clinics and wells to Central Luzon, while new government agencies assisted the tenant farmers, providing the sort of financial aid which the *Huks* could only promise.

One well publicized program involved the relocation of former *Huks* and their families on new land on the island of Mindanao, far from rebel-affected areas. Like the "New Villages" policy in Malaya, this successfully split the rebels from their supporters. Finally, with American assistance, the Filipino army was organized into small, self-sufficient Battalion

Burmese trooops in action against rebels, Insein, 1949

Combat Teams, and sent to rebel-affected areas to seek out and destroy remaining guerrilla bands.

In general terms, this pattern was not dissimilar to that of the British in Malaya: instead of treating the insurgency in purely military terms, Ramon Magsaysay had recognized the essentially political nature of the problem, concentrating on gaining popular support for the existing government and isolating the active guerillas from the people. It proved to be successful.

The *Huks* were forced onto the defensive and by 1954 some 9,695 had been killed, 1,635 wounded and 4,269 captured. In addition, no less than 15,866 had surrendered, including Taruc himself. Magsaysay went on to become president of the Philippines in November 1953 and, by the time of his death in a plane crash in March 1957, the *Huk* uprising had been completely broken. A brief revival between 1965 and 1970, led by Taruc's nephew, made very little impact.

Burma

The mixture of communist and purely nationalist groups that was such a feature of the *Huk* revolt was also apparent in Burma. On January 4, 1948, Britain granted independence to a new Union of Burma made up of five states – Chin, Kachim, Karen, Kayah and Shan – and led by the Anti-Fascist People's Freedom League (AFPFL). However, the hill tribes refused to cooperate with the central government.

Within less than two months of independence, Burma faced near chaos, starting with a civil war that broke out between the AFPFL and its communist partners. The "Red Flags" group of the Burmese Communist Party had left the government in February 1946 and, with the Muslim Mujahids, launched a revolt in the western coastal province of Arakan. The remaining "White Flags" group, previously expelled from the AFPFL, tried to mount an uprising in the Pegu area in March 1948.

The Karen uprising

The situation soon became extremely confused as more and more armed groups tried to seize local power. In particular, the Karens, who had wished to remain outside the Union, formed the Karen National Defense Organization (KNDO) and occupied the town of Moulmein for two months. After an attempt at a settlement had failed, Burmese President U Nu decided to take a much stronger line, authorizing the raising of paramilitary *Sitwundans* or territorial units. These carried out several massacres of Karen Christians in December 1948 and early 1949. The KNDO retaliated and bitter fighting broke out.

The chaos increased with a rising among "White Band" elements of the People's Volunteer Organization, and the mutiny of three battalions of the Burma Rifles around Prome. The government became isolated, depending for its survival upon the equally unreliable armed forces that remained. When elements of the Karen Rifles started fighting other government forces in January 1949, the Burmese authorities were faced with up to 37,000 insurgents. The chances of survival seemed slim particularly as the situation was clearly too complex for the introduction of counter-insurgency techniques. By 1949, the Burmese government was facing open revolt and civil war.

The Burmese government regains control

However, because the various groups were never coordinated, the government could fight each individually in a series of campaigns that continued well into the 1950s. Nonetheless, the insurgents managed to close the Rangoon-to-Mandalay road for three years, to control vital oilfields and mines and to disrupt river traffic on both the Sittang and Irrawaddy. The most formidable group was the Karens, who seized Mandalay, Insein, Meiktila, Maymyo and the Mawchi mines, and their attack on Rangoon was only defeated by hastily improvised defenses that included an old armored car, home-made artillery and ex-British tanks salvaged from scrap heaps.

This marked something of a turning-point. The government was able to retain control of the rice revenues, and its monopoly of the few aircraft available eventually turned the tide between March and May 1949. The Karen revolt subsided into guerrilla war, although the government could not finish the job, being forced to deal with *Kuomintang* units entering the northeast of the country as they withdrew from the communist advances in China.

Karen guerrillas on the march in eastern Burma.

Burmese government forces recaptured the Mawchi mines from the Karens in November 1953, depriving them of their major source of money, and when a degree of local autonomy was offered to the Karens in exchange for an end to the fighting, many guerrillas accepted the terms. Karen leader Mahn Ba Zan remained at large – indeed, Karen rebels still occupied frontier areas in the southeast until May 1980, when amnesty terms were finally accepted – but the threat to the central authorities had subsided by then.

Burma was the most complex of the postwar conflicts, but at least the nationalists had been given independence peacefully and had not faced a coordinated communist insurgency. The Burmese government survived the many long conflicts but was left politically and economically weak. Furthermore, the splits within Burmese society were not healed by government "victory," leaving the country unstable. As early as 1958, elements of the armed services took over the government, while countercoups in 1962 and 1974, the latter of which was unsuccessful, merely reinforced the spiral of violence. Despite apparently strong central control exercised by the army and its political followers, ethnic differences, fueled by the continued presence of Chinese dissidents in the north (where the trade in heroin offers enormous wealth and power), have continued to create unrest.

Indonesian independence

In the case of Indonesia, all the previously-noted sources of conflict, from anticolonialism to communist insurgency and regional instability, came together in the immediate postwar period. As in Indochina, the problems began as soon as the Japanese surrendered in 1945, for despite a declaration of independence by the nationalists, British troops landed in Java on September 29 to prepare the way for a Dutch return. But the British, in common with the Americans and Australians, recognized the force of nationalist demands and urged the Dutch to negotiate. This was especially the case after clashes with armed nationalists in Java.

The Dutch did indeed open negotiations with the Indonesians, but would not agree to total independence, preferring a system that would give them some continued control. Disputes arose over the definition and timing of partial independence until the Dutch demanded that their rule should continue until at least February 1949. On June 20, 1947, they launched a major "police action" on Java, Sumatra and Madura in an attempt to enforce this arrangement militarily.

Significant military success was achieved, but at the cost of alienating both Indonesian and Western opinion. Pressure from the United States and the newly established United Nations led to another agreement, based on the idea of a federal system. The nationalists believed that this was merely another way of preserving Dutch influence, and the fighting continued. In a second "police action" on December 18, 1948, Dutch Marines captured the nationalist capital of Djogjakarta in eastern Java, together with most of the nationalist leadership, including Sukarno.

However, this did nothing to improve the popularity of the Dutch, who soon faced a guerrilla war of increasing violence. Further American pressure, including a threat to stop economic assistance to the Netherlands, led to a final round of negotiations which resulted in a Dutch hand-over of power on November 2, 1949, and the emergence of a federal republic on August 17, 1950.

Dutch soldiers during the second "police action" in Indonesia, 1948.

Communist risings

Indonesia's new government immediately faced risings by rival factions now welded together into a federation. The first rising at Madiun, in September 1948, was the work of the veteran communist leader Musso, and although it was easily contained, it bred lasting hatred between the communists and the Indonesian armed forces, especially the army chief of staff, Abdul Nasution. Following Nasution's dismissal by Sukarno in 1962, communist influence in the government increased and, when Sukarno fell seriously ill, the communists attempted a coup on September 30, 1965, aiming to eliminate the army leadership. Six senior generals were murdered, but Nasution escaped to lead the army against the communist rebels. Estimates vary, but as many as 500,000 communists or suspected communists perished as the army seized effective control of the country and exacted its revenge. Political suppression and imprisonments were severe for some time thereafter.

The communist coup was itself a reflection of Sukarno's failure to harness the forces of Islam, Marxism and nationalism. Muslim risings took place in Java in 1949 and Sulawesi in 1953, while dissident officers had proclaimed and maintained a "revolutionary government" in Sumatra from 1958 to 1961.

Sukarno's attempts to expand and create a "Greater Indonesia" also brought disaster. There was opposition to Indonesian control of West Irian in 1963 and Sukarno miscalculated badly in his opposition to the creation of the Malaysian Federation, due to incorporate Malaya, Singapore, Brunei, Sarawak, and Sabah (although Brunei subsequently withdrew). From the beginning, Sukarno regarded the federation as a block to Indonesian expansion on the island of Borneo. When the sultanate of Brunei flared into revolt on December 8, 1962, Sukarno seized the opportunity of "smashing" Malaysia. He believed that the rising against the sultan, who favored federation, indicated opposition to Malaysia throughout northern Borneo.

Members of the Sarawak Police Force check enemy dead during the revolt in Brunei, December 1962.

CONFRONTATION, 1963–66

Malaysian Territory

Indonesian territory

Indonesian attacks on Sarawak and Sabah

SABAH
BRUNEI
SARAWAK
MALAYA
SULAWESI
WEST IRIAN
BORNEO
SUMATRA

0 Miles 400
0 Km 600

JAVA
MADURA

FLASHPOINTS DURING 1947–48

BATAVIA (JAKARTA)
MADURA
SURABAYA
JAVA
MADUIN
DJOGJAKARTA

✿ Flashpoints

Confrontation

Masterminded by the pro-Sukarno A. M. Azahari, and led in the field by Yassin Affendi, the 4,000 rebels in Brunei tried to seize key locations, including the sultan's palace, the country's power station and its oilfields. In fact, the authorities had received some prior warning and the rebels failed in their objectives. British troops were flown in from Singapore and the revolt had all but collapsed by December 14.

Many rebels fled into the jungle, closely pursued by the security forces, and Affendi was eventually captured on May 18, 1963. By then, however, Sukarno had announced that "volunteers" would liberate the northern part of Borneo (known to the Indonesians as Kalimantan Utara) and the first such group of armed men had crossed the frontier on April 12, 1963. Thus began what was known as the "Confrontation."

With only limited resources, the British commander in Borneo, Major-General Walter Walker, had to defend over 1,560 km (970 miles) of frontier and some 207,000 square kilometers (80,000 square miles) of jungle against Indonesian infiltration. The same techniques that had proved so successful in Malaya were again applied by the British, with a fully integrated command and intelligence structure, a well-organized "hearts and minds" campaign to win over the jungle people, the raising of local forces (such as the 1,500-strong Border Scouts) and highly flexible operations using helicopters, which had not been available in earlier counterinsurgency campaigns.

Having failed to prevent the establishment of Malaysia on September 16, 1963, Sukarno increased the scope of the action, committing regular Indonesian troops. British forces methodically extended their response to meet the new threat. By 1965, the Indonesians had been forced to abandon their forward positions along the border and had effectively surrendered the military initiative to the British. With his economy faltering under the strain of the conflict, Sukarno's popularity waned and, when he fell ill in August 1965, the army took the opportunity to end the Confrontation as soon as they had dealt with the communist coup. On August 11, 1966, military rulers under General Suharto made an agreement with Malaysia and, for the first time in over 20 years, Indonesia entered a comparatively settled period. However, Indonesia's problems continue. Suharto may be backed by a strong, army-controlled government, quite prepared to use force to suppress unrest, and there is no doubt that he has taken significant steps to improve the economy, stabilizing the currency and exploiting the advantages of oil, but with a rapidly growing population and a lack of political freedom, all the ingredients of revolt remain.

SEATO to ASEAN

Between 1945 and 1965, therefore, Southeast Asia experienced a wide variety of conflicts in its efforts to shake off colonial rule and assert its independence. In some cases, this had led to communist risings or even victories, so that although the region was possibly more settled by 1965, it had unavoidably entered the forefront of the global struggle between East and West. It had, in effect, exchanged its colonial past for a future dominated by the interests of the rival superpowers.

As early as September 1954, in an attempt to block further expansion by the communists, the Americans put together the Southeast Asia Treaty Organization (SEATO), in which the Philippines, Thailand, Pakistan, the United States, Australia, New Zealand, Britain and France agreed to take joint action in the event that any one of them was attacked in Southeast Asia. This was never particularly effective (it lapsed in 1975), as shown by the refusal of some of its key members to help the Americans in Vietnam ten years later. Its very existence, however, showed Southeast Asia's important place in the global balance of power.

The failure of SEATO, coupled with the growing fear that Southeast Asia was becoming a superpower battleground, led the main countries of the region to explore the idea of self-help, free from American or Soviet manipulation. Indonesia, for example, looked to the "Non-Aligned" movement, founded in April 1955. This movement has tried to pursue policies independent of those of the superpower blocs, but its influence has been mixed.

Of far more significance was the creation in 1967 of the Association of Southeast Asian Nations (ASEAN), in which Thailand, the Philippines, Malaysia, Singapore and Indonesia came together in an effort to further social and economic development. Since that date, some members have been pressing for a more military-orientated organization, and the appeal of such a local alliance has not waned. Nonetheless the continued presence of American and Soviet military and naval forces in the region suggests the difficulty of complete independence from the superpowers. In the light of American efforts in Vietnam between 1965 and 1973 and the continued spread of communism since that time, this is hardly surprising.

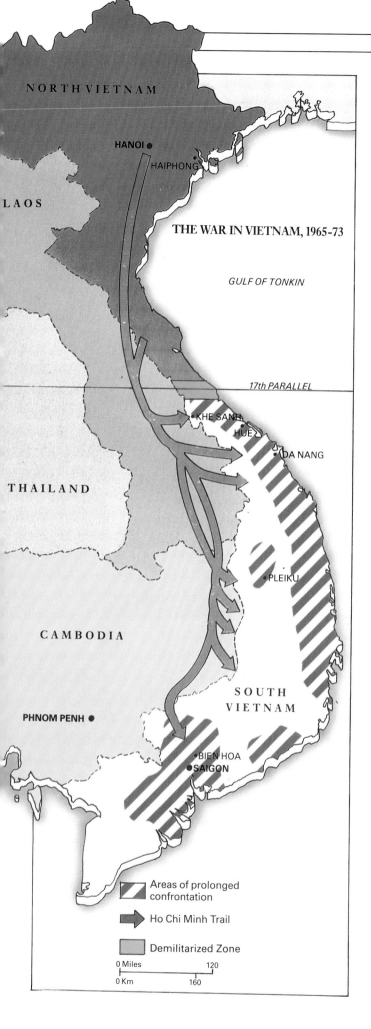

THE WAR IN VIETNAM, 1965-73

NORTH VIETNAM

HANOI

HAIPHONG

LAOS

GULF OF TONKIN

17th PARALLEL

KHE SANH
HUE
DA NANG

THAILAND

PLEIKU

CAMBODIA

SOUTH
VIETNAM

PHNOM PENH

BIEN HOA
SAIGON

Areas of prolonged
confrontation

Ho Chi Minh Trail

Demilitarized Zone

0 Miles — 120
0 Km — 160

CHAPTER 3
THE WAR IN VIETNAM, 1965-1975

For over a decade, the Vietnam War was the central drama on the Southeast Asian stage, and one with a global audience. As the North Vietnamese struggled to unify the country under communist rule, the United States became increasingly involved in its superpower role of combating the spread of communism. However, while the North Vietnamese were prepared to fight a total war, using all their resources to achieve final victory, the United States grew increasingly concerned at the cost of its involvement and the failure of its massive military power to win the war. Disillusionment gradually set in, fueled by widespread opposition to the war both inside America and among her allies, leading to negotiated withdrawal of United States forces in early 1973. Two years later, South Vietnam fell to the North and the communists took over in Laos and Cambodia. It was a major upheaval in Southeast Asia.

Following French withdrawal from Indochina, Vietnam was left in a political limbo which promised future conflict. North Vietnam would not renounce its objective of a united communist nation, and merely paused to organize its forces to continue the struggle. South Vietnam, unable to create a credible central government, could only survive with increasing American military backing.

The Geneva Agreements of July 21, 1954, which divided the country in half, offered few solutions. In theory, elections were to be held in 1956 to reunite north and south under a mutually acceptable national leader. The elections were never held. The fact that the majority of the population was in North Vietnam suggested to the United States and South Vietnam that any election would result in communist victory. In any event, the ruler of South Vietnam, Ngo Dinh Diem, did not feel himself bound by the Geneva agreement.

Diem takes over

At first the new republic of South Vietnam prospered with Diem deposing the former Emperor, Bao Dai, who had been installed as first president. The French left by April 1956 but the United States had already begun to offer assistance, seeing the fall of northern Vietnam as the latest in a long line of communist successes and determined to prevent a further spread of an ideology opposed to the capitalist, free enterprise, liberal democratic American ideal. During the later stages of the French involvement, American aid had been freely offered – by 1954 an estimated 80 per cent of the French war effort was being funded by Washington – and it was only natural that, once the advance of communism had been halted at the 17th parallel, the United States should step in to prevent any further spread into South Vietnam, Laos and Cambodia. Indochina, whether it liked it or not, was unavoidably in the front line of the "Cold War" between the rival superpower blocs.

When he took over in Saigon, Diem faced a number of problems, not least the fragmented nature of South Vietnamese society. A member of the traditional, Roman Catholic ruling elite, Diem had little contact with the ordinary peasants who, seeing him as merely the next in an established line of alien dictators, offered him no real support. He was able to establish control in Saigon and the provincial capitals, breaking the power

The face of communism. Viet Cong in action, Quang Tri.

of rival religious and criminal sects, but his rule was corrupt and dominated by members of his own family. He even tried to curb the power of the Buddhists, for long a major influence in peasant life.

Diem also faced the pressure of increasing communist activity and success. North Vietnam, backed economically and militarily by the Soviet Union and China, was building up its regular force, the North Vietnamese Army (NVA). At the same time, within South Vietnam, the guerrilla activities of the National Liberation Front, or Viet Cong, were being stepped up from 1957 onwards, pursuing a classic Maoist strategy. The Viet Cong was made up of *Viet Minh* veterans who had remained in the south after partition in 1954. They were increasingly supplemented by recruits and by NVA troops infiltrated from the north. NVA units and supplies for the Viet Cong were brought into the south via the Ho Chi Minh Trail, passing through Laos and Cambodia. Recognized by the North Vietnamese in 1960, the Viet Cong were soon estimated to control 60 per cent of the south.

The crisis deepens

There was also mounting communist insurgency in Laos and Cambodia. In the former country, one royal half-brother, Prince Souvana Phouma, had accepted both limited French autonomy in 1949 and subsequent independence in 1953. Another – Prince Souphanouvong – rejected it and established the Pathet Lao communist party with *Viet Minh* assistance. The two half-brothers had patched together a coalition in 1956 and agreed on Laotian neutrality but neither this, nor another neutrality agreement in 1962, prevented conflict. In neighboring Cambodia, Prince Sihanouk maintained a precarious independence amid mounting communist infiltration.

Diem came under increasing pressure, with two failed coups against him in 1960. Worried by the communist successes in the countryside, the new United States President, John F. Kennedy, sent General Maxwell Taylor to assess the situation in 1961. Taylor recommended a "massive joint effort" against the guerrillas, but because Laotian neutrality was still being negotiated, the US administration decided against dispatching combat troops. Instead the number of US advisers was increased and, in February 1962, the Military Assistance Command, Vietnam (MACV) was established. Also 5,000 US Marines were sent to Thailand in May 1962 in response to Pathet Lao pressure.

Diem falls from power

In the following year Buddhist hostility to Diem resulted in riots and demonstrations on the streets of South Vietnam and the appalling spectacle of Buddhist monks burning themselves to death. Government attacks on Buddhist pagodas disturbed the United States, who cut off assistance temporarily.

The Kennedy administration also gave some encouragement to an army coup against Diem on November 1, 1963, which resulted in the death of both Diem and his brother. However, there was little stability as regimes came and went over the next 18 months. At the end of 1964 Air Vice-Marshal Nguyen Cao Ky and General Nguyen Van Thieu finally brought political stability to Saigon. Ky was eventually replaced by Thieu, who remained in power until the fall of Vietnam in 1975, becoming president in September 1967. Like Diem before him, Thieu represented the established "elite," enjoying little understanding of peasant demands.

Increasing US involvement

By 1964, it was clear that the Saigon government could not hold the country in the face of Viet Cong successes and the United States would have to decide whether to commit itself to the defense of the south. Viet Cong tactics were based on the *Viet Minh* experience of fighting the French. In addition, they pursued a strategy of attacking government officials in order to expose Saigon's weakness. Over 11,000 people were abducted or killed in 1964 alone, and the South Vietnamese government's control in many areas of the countryside was shattered. Faced with this crisis, the number of US advisers was increased to over 23,000.

US involvement in Vietnam was by no means a foregone conclusion after the experience of the Korean War (1950-53). Opinion in the United States had been deeply divided over whether or not to intervene directly to assist the French in their war against the *Viet Minh* and, in the event, the Americans did not do so. Direct US military involvement in a war far from home, in which US strategic and economic interests were not self-evidently urgent, was even more controversial. The US government's public position rested on the "domino theory," that is, the idea that a communist take-over in one country would cause neighboring countries to topple into the communist camp. The appearance of a communist bloc in Southeast Asia would mean a tilt in the superpower balance in favor of the USSR or China.

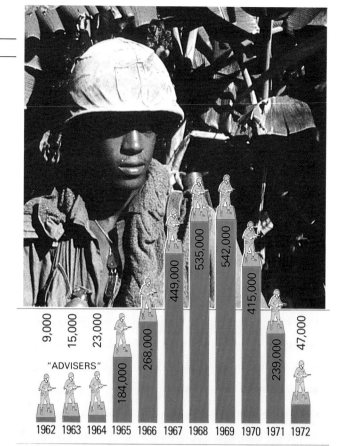

US TROOPS IN VIETNAM, 1962-1972

On August 2, 1964, the USS *Maddox*, on a surveillance mission in international waters in the Gulf of Tonkin, was attacked by three North Vietnamese torpedo boats. On the following day, another destroyer was also apparently attacked. As a result, President Lyndon B. Johnson, who had succeeded Kennedy on November 22, 1963, ordered bombing attacks against torpedo boat bases and oil-storage facilities in North Vietnam. On August 7, 1964, the US Congress, in a declaration known as the Gulf of Tonkin Resolution, gave the President wide powers to conduct war without further congressional approval. However, the fact that the Resolution was not an explicit declaration of war later gave grounds for questioning the legality of American operations.

Immediate US reaction was limited to 64 air raids on North Vietnamese targets. US policy remained uncertain, despite a Viet Cong attack on the American air base in Bien Hoa in October 1964. The President sent special assistant McGeorge Bundy to Saigon in January 1965 to make recommendations on increasing the US presence.

In the event, the issue was decided when the Viet Cong attacked US barracks at Pleiku on February 7, 1965, causing 100 American casualties. On the same day Johnson initiated new air raids on North Vietnam code-named Flaming Dart I and Flaming Dart II. On March 2, 1965, a major air offensive, Rolling Thunder, was launched and continued, with temporary interruptions, until October 31, 1968.

A B-52 Stratofortress bombs enemy positions in South Vietnam.

US tactics

Johnson coupled the bombing of the North with an offer of negotiations but the continued demoralization of the Army of the Republic of (South) Vietnam (ARVN) and the appearance of North Vietnamese (NVA) troops in the South confronted the President with crucial decisions. On March 8, 1965, US Marines landed at Da Nang to guard US air bases being used in the bombing offensive against the North.

The United States considered an "enclave strategy" where US troops would only protect their own bases and thus prevent the Viet Cong from winning the whole country. However, General William Westmoreland, who had become head of MACV in June 1964, believed that only US forces could fight the NVA. In fact the Americans made the mistake of believing that the NVA was a regular army when it was actually geared to waging guerrilla warfare. Thus, while the ARVN was left to tackle the Viet Cong, US troop strength increased steadily and was drawn into commitments farther from the bases as US forces pursued the elusive NVA. Westmoreland demanded and got his forces increased to 184,300 servicemen by the end of 1965.

Hanoi civil defense after US raid, August 1967.

US bombing

The problem was that the United States failed to find an effective way of using its vast technological resources in South Vietnam. The entire effort rested on too many mistaken assumptions about the aims of the communist leadership in Hanoi. It was assumed, for example, that the bombing of North Vietnam would force Hanoi into negotiations. In fact, bombing allowed the North Vietnamese to score a major propaganda victory in projecting an image of a small country confronted by a mighty war machine. Increasingly, bombing caused the United States itself political damage.

On the other hand, there were also doubts that Johnson's temporary halts to the bombing, such as between December 1965 and January 1966, would make the North Vietnamese negotiate rather than face further bombing. In any case, the bombing did not stop the flow of men and equipment into South Vietnam along the Ho Chi Minh Trail. Losses were soon made good by further supplies from China, the Soviet Union and the Eastern bloc.

The effectiveness of the bombing campaign was also limited by the Americans' decision, taken for political reasons, not to attack the only two worthwhile economic targets in North Vietnam – the Red River dikes and Haiphong harbor. Also although 2.4 million tons of bombs were dropped over the Trail in Laos between 1965 and 1971, US ground forces could not be committed to either Laos or Cambodia. Similarly, US ground forces could not be used across the 17th parallel, or Demilitarized Zone (DMZ).

A Ch-53 helicopter carries a 105mm howitzer over a US firebase.

Ground forces

In South Vietnam itself, the United States also assumed that it could dictate the war on the ground. The Americans believed they could achieve a relatively swift military victory, inflicting such heavy losses on the Viet Cong and NVA that they would give up the struggle. In reality, while the United States tried to wage a "limited" war, Hanoi pursued a "total" war in which any sacrifice could be accepted. The leadership in Hanoi, including Ho Chi Minh, until his death in 1969, and strategist Vo Nguyen Giap, was prepared to prolong the war until the United States lost its resolve.

Thus, the United States did not find its 47,000 dead an acceptable price to pay for the rescue of South Vietnam from communism while Hanoi was prepared for a final death toll estimated to be in excess of one million. Hanoi had no need to consider internal public opinion while the United States administration faced both international criticism and growing opposition to the war in the United States itself.

The failure to translate a degree of military success into political victory placed mounting pressure on the Johnson administration. In April 1967 Westmoreland requested either a "minimum essential force" of 550,000 to win the war within five years or an "optimum force" of 670,000 to finish it in three. He was told to make do with the troops he already had but attained the "minimum" figure – a peak strength of 542,000 US troops – in January 1969.

Even with larger numbers of troops, it is doubtful if the United States could have succeeded in South Vietnam. There was little effective coordination in command. Westmoreland was responsible to both naval and military chiefs of staff in the Pacific, and Washington interfered in the conduct of the war at all levels. Westmoreland had little control over the US Marines or air operations and was unable to establish a joint US-Vietnamese command in the face of Vietnamese reluctance. United States civilian agencies also took a hand in the war.

Pacification programs

The United States Army and Marines were ill-prepared for guerrilla conflict. Major bases were established throughout the country but, in contrast to the British in Malaya and Borneo, US operations were on a large scale. Also US troops were not keen to patrol the interior for prolonged periods. Indeed, troops rarely carried out ground operations which might result in casualties, and firepower came to be substituted for "feet on the ground." Inevitably, this increased the risk of civilian casualties.

Moreover, the United States failed to appreciate the need to wage a "hearts and minds" campaign, persuading the ordinary people to support the existing government in Saigon rather than the communists. Less than 10 per cent of US resources were devoted to this vital aspect of counterinsurgency and those efforts that were made – the rebuilding of shattered villages, the building up of trust between US advisers and local people, the use of pro-government propaganda – were often wasted as they were overwhelmed by the brute force of military response. The South Vietnamese started to resettle the rural population in 1959, for example, and, with the advice of a British Advisory Mission, this was expanded into a "Strategic Hamlets Program," but it bore little relation to the "New Villages" of Malaya.

Whereas just over 400 new villages had been constructed in 12 years in Malaya, over 6,000 strategic hamlets were built in the first year of the South Vietnamese program in 1962. By 1967, when the United States introduced its computerized Hamlet Evaluation System, there were over 12,750 strategic hamlets. Many lacked facilities and sufficient protection although both Regional Forces and Popular Forces were raised. There was also a *Chieu Hoi* (Open Arms) amnesty program to persuade Viet Cong guerrillas to change sides and a more controversial *Phuong Hoang* (Phoenix) program directed against the Viet Cong as a political organization. However, the increasingly impressive statistics of the number of South Vietnamese "won over" to the government lacked real meaning.

The South Vietnamese government was undeniably tainted with corruption. Land reform, which might have won popular support, was delayed until 1970. If there was little love for the communists, who manifestly failed to provoke a popular uprising during the Tet offensive of 1968, there was also little lasting support for the government in Saigon.

US riverboat crew returns fire during a Viet Cong attack in the Mekong Delta, June 1968.

The Tet offensive

It was the massive military defeat of the Viet Cong and NVA during Tet that proved the major turning point in United States resolve. After considerable internal disagreement, the communist leadership agreed to launch an all-out offensive to coincide with the lunar new year (Tet) in January 1968. In fact, Giap made the same mistake as in 1951 against the French, for large-scale operations gave the Americans the possibility of bringing the full weight of their firepower to bear for the first time.

The VC/NVA offensive began with a diversionary attack against the US base at Khe Sanh on January 21, 1968, followed by attacks on 36 provincial capitals, 64 district capitals and 5 cities by over 70,000 men. There were probably as many as 50,000 communist casualties and pockets of resistance were swiftly dealt with everywhere except in Saigon and Hue. The commun-ists were finally defeated in Hue on February 25, 1968, and the siege of Khe Sanh was lifted on April 14, 1968.

In military terms it was a massive defeat for Giap. However, on the television screens of the United States Tet turned to victory. Images of the Viet Cong breaking into the supposedly impregnable US Embassy com-pound in Saigon made a profound impact on its audience. American public opinion, used to the idea of military "victory," found it hard to accept that the war in Vietnam was being fought not to destroy commun-ism but to contain it. As casualties among American forces increased, young men resisted conscription, opposition to the continuation of the war developed into a mass protest movement and government policies – especially the aerial bombardment of North Vietnam – came in for serious question, particularly by the media and by politicians of all parties.

Faced with this mounting antiwar opposition, Johnson decided not to run for reelection in the November presidential contest and offered new nego-tiations with another pause in the bombing offensive. Some progress was made and Johnson announced a complete halt to bombing on October 31, 1968, with peace talks to begin in Paris on the day after the American elections.

Refugees return to ruined city of Hue, March 1968.

THE TET OFFENSIVE, 1968

QUANG TRI
HUE
KHE SANH
A SHAU
DA NANG
HOI AN
KHAM DUC
LAOS
QUANG NGAI
DAK TOU
KONTUM
PLEIKU
ANKHE
QUI NHON
HAU BON
CAMBODIA
BAN ME THUOT
NHA TRANG
DALAT
SOUTH VIETNAM
AN LOC
BIEN HOA
PHAN THIET
SAIGON
CHAU PHU
VIN LONG
MYTHO
CAN THO
BEN TRE
RACH GIA
CAN THO
CA MAU

☆ Major assaults by VC/NVA

Demilitarized Zone

Areas of prolonged confrontation

Ho Chi Minh Trail

U Miles   100
0 Km   150

The Siege of Khe Sanh

The US combat base at Khe Sanh, in the extreme northwest of South Vietnam, was designed to act as a block to North Vietnamese advances along Route 9. In January 1968, as two North Vietnamese divisions prepared to attack, the base and its surrounding hills were held by the US 26th Marines.

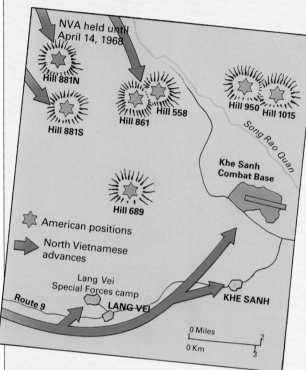

- NVA held until April 14, 1968
- Hill 881N
- Hill 881S
- Hill 861
- Hill 558
- Hill 950
- Hill 1015
- Song Rao Quan
- Khe Sanh Combat Base
- Hill 689

⭐ American positions

➡ North Vietnamese advances

Lang Vei Special Forces camp
LANG VEI
KHE SANH
Route 9

0 Miles | 2
0 Km | 3

CH-53 helicopter hit by NVA mortar near Khe Sanh airstrip.

On January 21, 1968, the North Vietnamese attacked Khe Sanh, advancing along Route 9 and into the hills to the north. The combat base was hit by a deluge of artillery fire which was to last for 70 days, but the Marines held firm. Despite the loss of Lang Vei and Hill 881N, the US defenders, backed by massive air power, prevented an enemy breakthrough.

NVA rockets exploding in Khe Sanh, February 1968.

Nixon's balancing act

In November 1968, Richard M. Nixon was elected president, promising "peace with honor." A respectable withdrawal involved the "Vietnamization" of the war, a policy of building up the ARVN so that it could gradually take over operations from the US forces which could then be brought home in phases.

Nixon's policy also involved a risky process of negotiating with the North Vietnamese while maintaining military pressure. In the event Nixon believed that he could only achieve peace by widening the war when necessary, above all by attacking NVA infiltration routes in Cambodia and Laos.

In March 1970 the Prime Minister of Cambodia, Lon Nol, deposed Prince Norodom Sihanouk. The Americans welcomed Lon Nol as a man who was likely to cooperate with Saigon in the destruction of Viet Cong bases in Cambodian territory, and Sihanouk responded by joining the communist Khmer Rouge. The fighting in Cambodia quickly spread, fueled by the fact that Nixon had allowed widespread secret bombing against the communist supply lines in Cambodia.

On April 29, 1970, ARVN troops with US support advanced into Cambodia to attack Viet Cong and NVA bases and supply dumps. The operation provoked nationwide demonstrations in the United States. In May 1970, during one of these protests, four students were shot dead by National Guardsmen at Kent State University in Ohio and the antiwar movement built up to a new peak.

Congress decided to reassert its authority by repealing the Gulf of Tonkin Resolution on June 24 and passing an amendment on June 30 which prohibited US troops from entering Cambodia. By then, it was too late. The invading South Vietnamese had gone on the rampage against their traditional Khmer enemies, regardless of the latter's anti-communist leanings. Cambodia became a battleground.

American morale

By the end of 1971 it was clear that US forces could no longer be very effective. The total in Vietnam had declined to some 239,000. US morale in South Vietnam all but disintegrated with staggering increases in incidents of desertion, drug abuse, "fragging" (the murder of officers by fragmentation grenade), racial clashes and crime.

To some extent US servicemen were affected by antiwar propaganda from the United States. However, the main reasons for the decline in morale were internal to the armed forces. There was conflict between conscripts or "draftees" and professional soldiers as well as the failure of officers at all levels to exercise leadership qualities. Given such difficulties and the failure of Vietnamization to increase ARVN efficiency, Giap mounted a major conventional offensive against South Vietnam in March 1972.

The renewed bombing of North Vietnam

Once more, the "spring offensive" proved a major communist defeat as Nixon unleashed US air power for the first time since November 1968. On April 2, 1972, the United States again attacked North Vietnamese targets, and each time the negotiations at Paris became bogged down, Nixon increased the pressure. This time there were few restrictions and the Linebacker I operation achieved impressive results. Nixon halted the campaign on October 23, 1972.

Once again the North Vietnamese leadership dragged their feet over negotiations and on December 19 a 12-day campaign known as Linebacker II struck at Hanoi and Haiphong. Nixon halted the bombing once more on December 30, 1972, and an agreement for a ceasefire was concluded on January 9, 1973.

The speed of the final NVA conquest of South Vietnam took everyone by surprise. In Saigon there was chaos as people readied themselves for an uncertain future. Many expected a bloodbath.

The fall of South Vietnam

Nixon's only real aim was to withdraw US troops with honor and little was done to ensure the future security of South Vietnam. Though Nixon promised that US airpower would be used if the North Vietnamese attacked, in fact US assistance was further cut back by Congress and Nixon himself fell from office in August 1974 over the Watergate scandal. Investigation of an attempt to bug the Democratic Party headquarters in the Watergate apartments during the 1972 presidential campaign had led to the discovery of widespread irregularities in the Nixon administration. In the political uncertainty following the scandal, Nixon's successor, Gerald Ford, could do little to help the increasingly beleagured South Vietnamese.

In South Vietnam, Thieu's government was becoming more unpopular. The ARVN was short of equipment, especially fuel. The majority of the ARVN were unwilling conscripts and desertion was rife. The leadership in Hanoi was determined to reunite the country and by 1975 there were 12 NVA divisions in South Vietnam.

There had never been any real ceasefire in many areas and the bulk of the ARVN was positioned in the northern provinces. Thus, an NVA attack in the thinly defended Phuoc province, northeast of Saigon, caught the South Vietnamese by surprise in early 1975. The province was lost and the communists were encouraged by the lack of US reaction. In March 1975 Hanoi ordered a general offensive. Thieu abandoned the northern provinces but this caused a total collapse in the Central Highlands. The communists had not expected victory before 1976 but the whole of South Vietnam crumbled before them.

Thieu resigned as president on April 21, 1975, in favor of General Duong Van Minh who, it was hoped, might be able to negotiate, but the North Vietnamese refused to compromise. As the United States hastily tried to get their people out, Saigon fell on April 30, 1975. A war which had lasted 30 years – ever since Ho Chi Minh's declaration of independence in September 1945 – was over and Vietnam, for the first time in modern history, was ruled by one central government. The cost had been enormous: an estimated three million people had died (including 47,000 American servicemen), huge areas had been devastated and untold millions of people had seen their lives changed.

More importantly, North Vietnamese victory represented a major blow to American prestige and a boost to the cause of communism, particularly as, only 13 days before, Phnom Penh, Cambodia's capital, had fallen to the communist Khmer Rouge. A similar takeover occurred in Laos in June 1975, with Prince Souphanouvong becoming president of a communist People's Democratic Republic of Laos in December. A new era in Indochinese history had begun.

Unprepared for defeat, the Americans left many former allies behind. Evacuation of Nha Trang, February 1975.

Kampuchean refugees near the Thai border.

CHAPTER 4
VICTIMS OF PEACE

Communist victories in South Vietnam, Laos and Cambodia did little to reduce the levels of violence in Southeast Asia. Old territorial rivalries, held in check during the period of communist struggle, were revived in Indochina. The situation was further complicated as the Soviet Union and the People's Republic of China vied for influence in Southeast Asia. Clashes led to the occupation by Soviet-backed Vietnam of Chinese-backed Kampuchea (Cambodia), which in turn led to fighting between Vietnam and China itself. Continued violence within non-communist countries, in both the Philippines and Indonesia, also shows that the pattern of conflict imposed on Southeast Asia as a whole since 1945 is unlikely to be broken.

The wars in Indochina between 1945 and 1975 have tended to dominate the postwar history of Southeast Asia, not merely because of their huge cost in human lives (an estimated three million dead) but also because of the American involvement. However, Indochina has had to suffer the violent aftermath of its long struggle, while superpower interests have continued to dominate Southeast Asian affairs.

The new Indochina

As the new communist regimes in South Vietnam, Laos and Kampuchea imposed their rule in Indochina, many thousands of ordinary people suffered, among the first being the people of Indochina who had supported the old regimes. In Vietnam, there were reports of summary executions of captured anti-communist leaders, while all former officials and soldiers of the Thieu regime were forced to register with the communists. Prominent supporters were sent to special reeducation camps, where they faced an often brutal period of forced labor, inadequate food and political indoctrination, designed to make them see the "error of their ways."

It has been suggested that up to 200,000 people may have been imprisoned in this way in 1977 and it is possible that over 50,000 still remain, although the Vietnamese claimed that 90 per cent had been released by March 1978. Less important officials and soldiers were given lesser doses of the same treatment, while the southern population as a whole was closely supervised and subjected to endless pro-communist propaganda. Special "people's revolutionary committees" were set up in the villages, anti-communist religions such as Buddhism and Roman Catholicism were persecuted, any signs of resistance were ruthlessly crushed and all symbols of Western culture, from long hair to fashions, were attacked.

Socialist transformation

The communists were also intent on imposing "socialist transformation" in the economy and politics of their new areas of control. For example, a "Five-Year Plan" begun in December 1976 involved sending city-dwellers from the south of Vietnam into the country to "rediscover" their peasant roots and contribute to the agricultural recovery of a devastated land.

Some 700,000 people were forced to leave Saigon (renamed Ho Chi Minh City) by June 1977 and by the following January it was estimated that 1.3 million people had been "relocated" in special "economic zones" in rural areas. In the process, they suffered hardship, not merely because of their unsuitability for the work but also because the communists could not cope with the inevitable demands for food, shelter and disease prevention. At the same time, in an effort to destroy the business class that had grown up in the south to serve the American presence, a new currency was introduced and the traditional trading patterns of the country were deliberately disrupted.

The boat people

These changes affected the country's Chinese population particularly, and many fled to avoid persecution. A significant number – some 675,000 – trekked north to cross the border into China itself, but others could only escape by sea. At least 10 per cent of these so-called "boat people" may have died in the process through drowning, exposure or attacks by pirates, but huge numbers soon began to arrive in other countries of the region (and beyond), clamoring for aid. By July 1979, 120,000 refugees had landed in Malaysia, 11,000 in the Philippines, 40,000 in Indonesia, 2,100 in Singapore, 30,000 in Thailand and still more in Hong Kong.

Many of these countries suspected that the Vietnamese authorities were conducting a deliberate policy of encouraging the mass emigration of people who might cause trouble if they remained. In July 1979 a conference at Geneva managed to persuade the Vietnamese to stop the flow. However, a new purge of Chinese in the spring of 1984 led to a reported 250,000 additional refugees.

One of the many worn-out boats full of Vietnamese refugees to arrive in Hong Kong, 1979.

The Cambodian nightmare

Nor was this a pattern of events confined to Vietnam, for in Cambodia, or Democratic Kampuchea as it was renamed in December 1975, the communists were even more ruthless. The Khmer Rouge announced that they were unable to guarantee the security or food supplies of the 2.5 million inhabitants of Phnom Penh when it fell and forced the entire population to leave within eight days. Over the next few months, the new regime sent 3.5 million city-dwellers and 500,000 country people by force to "new villages," where they faced malnutrition, hard labor, disease and seemingly mindless violence.

Indeed, the Khmer Rouge under Pol Pot's irrational leadership made little attempt to "reeducate" the masses, preferring simply to kill off anyone who might oppose their views. For a time, it was dangerous to be seen wearing spectacles – a sign of a Western-style education – and young children were used as informers against their own families. The number of people who died will probably never be accurately known, but it is possible that as many as 1.4 million perished from starvation, disease or execution by January 1977.

The Kampuchean terror inevitably produced yet more refugees. By April 1976, between 30,000 and 50,000 had crossed into Thailand from Kampuchea, a figure that had risen to 150,000 by August 1979. By then, an additional 321,000 had fled into Vietnam, many of them ethnic Vietnamese, and the situation steadily worsened as the Vietnamese invasion of Kampuchea, initiated in December 1978, increased the pressures on the local population. By the end of 1980, the refugees in Thailand or along its borders numbered some 620,000 – a figure which had not altered significantly four years later – and the Thai authorities, worried about security, were finding it difficult to cope.

Vietnam and Kampuchea

Armed conflict with superpower involvement returned to the region in the late 1970s, with full-scale war between Vietnam and Kampuchea. The flight of the Chinese from Vietnam and of the Vietnamese from Kampuchea were examples of traditional tensions between different ethnic groups. To some extent, these had been overshadowed by the struggle between communism and its opponents up to 1975. However, once the new regimes had been established in Indo-china, the old pattern of conflicts reemerged. Some of these were made worse by territorial disputes dating

Phnom Penh: money is worthless under the Khmer Rouge.

back to colonial times – the French, for example, had arbitrarily transferred some Khmer areas to Cochin China (in Vietnam) – but the Khmers were also suspicious of Vietnamese intentions generally.

Indeed, cooperation between the two groups had been bad even during the time when both were fighting for the common goal of communism. The Khmers found it difficult to forgive the Vietnamese for negotiating peace in 1954 and 1973 without allowing any concessions to the Khmer Rouge. In addition, the Vietnamese had made constant use of Cambodian territory during the war, occupying border zones which they showed no intention of giving up.

Under Pol Pot possibly a third of all Kampucheans died.

The Vietnamese themselves feared that Khmer policies, particularly under Pol Pot, would disrupt the sensitive border areas, where many of the new "economic zones" were situated. Moreover, the two sides made efforts to involve their superpower allies – the Soviet Union in the case of Vietnam and China in the case of Kampuchea – so opening the region to the possibility of a fresh round of interstate violence.

The Vietnamese invasion of Kampuchea

There were clashes between Vietnamese and Khmer forces as early as 1974, but the real crisis began in April 1977, when Khmer units advanced some 10 km (6 miles) into Vietnam, accusing the government in Hanoi of interfering in the internal politics of Kampuchea. A second major assault carried the Khmers a further 150 km (90 miles) into Vietnam in September 1977. At first, the Vietnamese responded by trying to contain the problem, but on December 31, 1977 they retaliated by sending six divisions (about 60,000 men) into Kampuchea, seizing river crossings only 56 km (35 miles) from Phnom Penh.

However, the Vietnamese claimed that this was only a warning and withdrew, offering to set up a demilitarized zone on the border in February 1978. Pol Pot rejected this, having severed diplomatic relations with Hanoi in December 1977, and there were further clashes throughout 1978. At this point, the Vietnamese resolved to take more decisive action.

On December 3 a former officer in the Khmer Rouge, Heng Samrin, was named by the Vietnamese as head of a Kampuchean National United Front for National Salvation (KNUFNS) and, on the 25th, 20,000 KNUFNS troops and 120,000 Vietnamese invaded Kampuchea. Pol Pot anticipated the attack, withdrawing some 60,000 of his soldiers to prepared jungle bases, and on January 3, 1979 Radio Phnom Penh announced that the Khmer Rouge would wage a guerrilla war, leaving the cities to the Vietnamese. Phnom Penh fell to the invaders on January 7 and Heng Samrin was installed as head of state of a new People's Republic of Kampuchea. Casualties may have amounted to 30,000 on each side.

China against Vietnam

The fall of Kampuchea had an immediate effect on relations between China and Vietnam. Conflict between these countries had long been brewing, for although China had supported the North Vietnamese for some time after 1949, the two countries had drifted

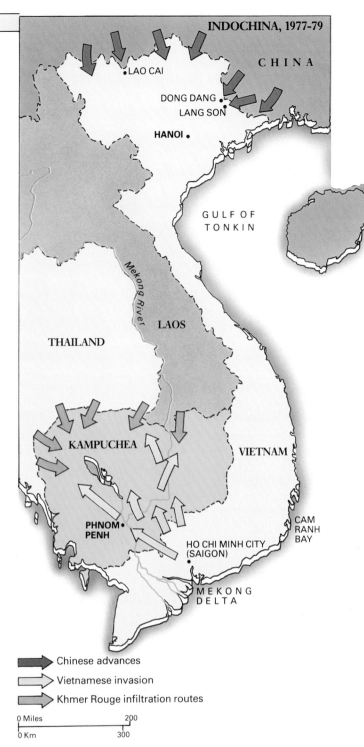

INDOCHINA, 1977-79

Chinese advances

Vietnamese invasion

Khmer Rouge infiltration routes

0 Miles — 200
0 Km — 300

apart as relations between China and the United States improved in the early 1970s.

This had forced the Vietnamese to look for aid to the Soviet Union, which had a long-running rivalry with China. The Vietnamese invasion of Kampuchea convinced China that Vietnam was being used as a tool of Soviet expansion on her southern borders. As a result, the authorities in Peking felt they had to support Pol Pot to maintain their influence in the area, despite the international condemnation he attracted and the fact that he ignored Chinese advice.

Diplomatic relations

The flight of the boat people, largely ethnic Chinese, increased the tension. When Vietnam joined Comecon, the Soviet economic organization, in June 1978, China cut off all economic aid (worth $30 million annually), withdrew its technicians and recalled its ambassador from Hanoi. Talks were held on the refugee problem but failed to find a solution, and any hopes the Chinese may have had that economic pressure would prevent a Vietnamese invasion of Kampuchea were soon dashed. In reality, such policies merely pushed the Vietnamese closer to the Soviets, with whom they concluded a treaty of peace and friendship on November 3, 1978. The Chinese responded by opening full diplomatic relations with the United States.

The Chinese invasion

Such an obvious breakdown of relations made some sort of clash inevitable, and throughout 1978 Vietnamese and Chinese forces fought minor actions on the border between the two states. But it was the Vietnamese invasion of Kampuchea which brought matters to a head, for as soon as this occurred, the Chinese began to talk openly of teaching Vietnam a "lesson" and "punishing" her aggression. On February 17, 1979, Chinese forces invaded northern Vietnam, advancing towards Lao Cai and Dong Dang with an army of approximately 80,000 men.

However, the lack of recent Chinese combat experience began to show – they had not fought a major war since that in Korea (1950-53) – and, as casualties mounted, they were forced to commit even greater numbers, up to an estimated 200,000. They managed to take Lang Son on March 2, 1979 and went on to occupy four provincial capitals in the north. However, it soon became apparent that the main aim of the operation – to force the Vietnamese to withdraw troops from Kampuchea – had not been achieved. On March 16, rather than face the prospect of a lengthy war of attrition, the Chinese withdrew, announcing that their "punishment" was complete.

Vietnamese domination of Indochina

The fact that this was ineffective may be shown by the continued Vietnamese occupation of Kampuchea and their virtual domination of the countries of Indochina. By 1979, Vietnam had an estimated 50,000 men in Laos and 200,000 in Kampuchea and her army was the most powerful in Southeast Asia. She signed a treaty with Laos in August 1977 and another with Heng Samrin of Kampuchea in February 1979, and in more recent years there have been signs that she has been trying to extend her influence into Burma.

All of this has, of course, affected Thailand, increasing security fears. The Khmer Rouge made some advances into Thai territory in 1976 and 1977 and, since 1979, the Vietnamese have accused the Thais of harboring Khmer guerrillas. Thai and Vietnamese forces have clashed during each dry season (October to April) since 1980, and the Thai-Laotian border was closed in February 1981.

The Chinese Army in action on the Vietnamese border, April 1978.

On the Thai-Kampuchean border, the situation is further complicated by the presence of other, non-communist, forces alongside the Khmer Rouge guerrillas. A former Cambodian prime minister, Son Sann, founded a Khmer People's National Liberation Front (KPNLF) with some 6,000 to 13,000 men. Prince Sihanouk still leads a *Moulinaka* movement with perhaps 5,000 supporters. In June 1983, these groups joined forces with the 35,000 to 50,000 Khmer Rouge to form a somewhat fragile Coalition Government of Democratic Kampuchea, headed by Sihanouk with Son Sann as prime minister. By then, the Khmers had replaced Pol Pot with Khieu Samphan and had abandoned their Marxist organization in an attempt to win international recognition.

To a large extent, this has succeeded, since the Khmer Rouge are still deemed to occupy the Kampuchean seat at the United Nations. Indeed, in May 1981 they were still recognized by a total of 84 states (out of a UN membership of 157). As a result, the UN General Assembly has condemned Vietnamese occupation of Kampuchea on a number of occasions. The Vietnamese in turn have organized elections in Kampuchea and have announced partial troop withdrawals in July 1982, April 1983 and June 1984, but they have shown no real signs of leaving the country.

Continuing tensions

Fighting has continued inside Kampuchea, and the Vietnamese offensive during the 1984-85 dry season was the largest to date, involving the reported capture of 13 guerrilla bases. Accurate information is hard to come by, but it would appear that Son Sann no longer leads the KPNLF, having been deposed in January 1986, although this does not seem to have affected the conduct of the guerrilla war.

The continued fighting means that the threat of Vietnamese interference in Thailand is still present, and it is interesting to note that this has led to pressures for military action among the members of the Association of Southeast Asian Nations (ASEAN). One effect of all this has been to isolate Vietnam within Southeast Asia and that, in turn, has led to increased dependence by the Vietnamese upon the Soviet Union. By 1979, the Soviets and their Comecon partners were giving Vietnam economic aid to the tune of $2 million a day, in return for which some 80,000 Vietnamese were working in the Soviet Union and base facilities for Soviet naval vessels had been made available at Cam Ranh Bay.

Meanwhile, there has been continuing tension on the border between China and Vietnam, with the Chinese reporting a steady series of minor clashes, and more serious fighting in May/June 1981 and March/April 1984. The Chinese can do little beyond giving support to resistance movements inside Vietnam, Laos and Kampuchea, so a balance of sorts has been achieved. However, the threat of major conflict between China and Vietnam drawing in the Soviet Union (and the United States) shows just how delicate relations are within Southeast Asia.

Filipino conflict

Problems of internal ethnic and political unrest and of superpower strategic interest are not confined to Indochina. Since 1975 both the Philippines and Indonesia, with Western orientated, strong-arm regimes, have faced prolonged internal conflict.

In the Philippines, the island of Mindanao was the main center of confrontation, forcing the president, Ferdinand Marcos, to impose martial law between September 1972 and January 1981.

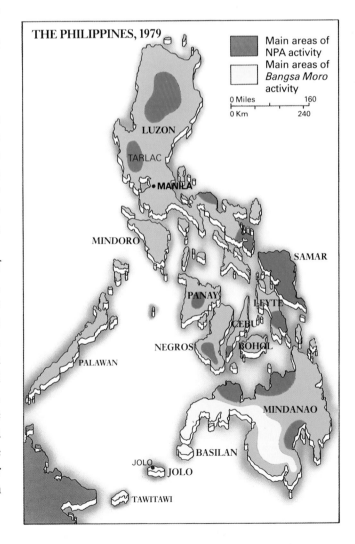

THE PHILIPPINES, 1979

Main areas of NPA activity

Main areas of *Bangsa Moro* activity

0 Miles 160
0 Km 240

LUZON

TARLAC

MANILA

MINDORO

SAMAR

PANAY

LEYTE

CEBU

NEGROS

BOHOL

PALAWAN

MINDANAO

BASILAN

JOLO

JOLO

TAWITAWI

Filipino guerrillas

The Islamic group known as the Moro Liberation Front and its military wing, *Bangsa Moro*, representing the resentment that existed between the strongly Moslem inhabitants of the southern islands and the Roman Catholic rulers in Manila, responded to this by initiating a campaign of guerrilla warfare which enjoyed some success. Marcos was forced to accept the principle of self-government, although he did avoid having to carry this out by insisting that all the people of the Philippines vote on the agreement, knowing full well that the Moros were in a minority.

Fighting broke out again in October 1977. Since then, the Moro movement has split, with different factions looking for assistance to Islamic countries as far away as Egypt, Libya and Saudi Arabia. Some have even approached the communists, represented by the New People's Army (NPA), active in the old *Huk* area of Tarlac province since 1969, although this has alienated some of the Moro activists, a proportion of whom surrendered to the Marcos regime rather than be associated with such extremist politics.

Indeed, many commentators now regard the communist threat to be the more threatening, for since the late 1970s the NPA – the military wing of the Maoist Communist Party of the Philippines, Marxist-Leninist – has increased its influence and popular support.

Forced to move its main base to Isabela province, northeast Luzon, in 1970, the NPA followed the Maoist pattern of revolution, gradually building a web of political support which kept it strong enough to fill the vacuum left by the Moro split in the late 1970s. By 1984 the NPA was estimated to consist of 11,000 activists and the United States was openly expressing fears of yet another communist victory in Southeast Asia. These fears were all the more urgent because of the key role played by US bases in the Philippines in America's strategic presence in Southeast Asia.

Nevertheless, the response of the central government did not differ according to the nature of the threat, and both Moro and New People's Army guerrilla groups have suffered the full force of military action by police, army and paramilitary units. Since 1972, between 50,000 and 100,000 people have died in these struggles, contributing to a record of violence and instability in the Philippines.

The fall of President Marcos

When first elected in 1965, Marcos had seemed an energetic and capable democrat whose main aim was to build a "New Society" in the Philippines. Unfortunately, this was undermined, partly by the actions of the various guerrilla groups, but also by the personal ambition and greed of Marcos himself.

Left: Members of the Bangsa Moro *Army prepare an ambush, July 1984.*

Below: The killing of Benigno Aquino at Manila Airport, August 1983.

The Aquinos

Reelected for a second term in 1969, he should not have been eligible for further elections thereafter according to the constitution, but the imposition of martial law allowed him to remain in power and even when the emergency was declared over in 1981 he merely changed the constitution to clear the way for a third term in office.

At the same time, Marcos and his wife Imelda were both considered to be involved in political corruption, using their positions to buy support and advance their own interests. In August 1983, the leader of the main opposition party, Benigno Aquino, was assassinated as soon as he stepped onto Filipino soil after a period of exile in the United States. A number of members of the armed forces, including the chief of staff, General Fabian Ver, were acquitted of responsibility in a trial in 1985, but Marcos was widely held to blame.

He was unperturbed by this and called for elections to be held in February 1986, despite the fact that his presidency still had a year to run. Almost immediately Aquino's widow, Mrs. Corazon Aquino, declared that she should stand against Marcos and, although she lacked any real experience of politics, the opposition parties rallied behind her. In the elections held on February 7, 1986, there was strong evidence that Marcos supporters had interfered with the voting, and when it was announced that Marcos had won, Mrs. Aquino called for a campaign of civil disobedience.

On February 22 the defense minister and the acting chief of staff to the armed forces both resigned from the government, taking refuge in the defense ministry building in Manila. By then, the United States – traditionally a supporter of Marcos, especially in his opposition to the communists in the Philippines – began to exert pressure on its ally and, amid street demonstrations, Marcos fled into exile on February 25, allowing Mrs. Aquino to assume the presidency.

This was certainly a popular move and one that led to more settled politics in the capital, but the Philippines still face the problems of armed action by the Moro and New People's Army groups, none of which accepted offers of ceasefire made by Mrs. Aquino. The potential for renewed crisis, with all its implications concerning American interests and the regional balance, is still there.

Mass demonstrations in Manila during February 1986 led to the peaceful overthrow of Marcos.

Indonesian problems

In Indonesia violence has been concentrated in the former Portuguese colony of East Timor, claimed by the government in Jakarta as part of Indonesia. The crisis began in April 1974, when the Portuguese dictator Marcello Caetano was overthrown in a military coup, for the new government immediately announced that all Portuguese colonies would be given their independence. In East Timor, this led to fighting between different groups of nationalists. When the Portuguese eventually left in August 1975, it was the *Frente Revolucionária Timorense de Libertação e Independência* (Revolutionary Front for the Liberation and Independence of Timor, usually shortened to *Fretilin*) that seized power.

The Indonesians responded by sending "volunteers" to invade the new country on December 7, 1975, and on August 14, 1976, they announced that East Timor was to be absorbed into Indonesia as Loro Sae province. A guerrilla war between *Fretilin* and the Indonesian occupation force has continued ever since, with undisclosed casualties, and although the Indonesians have offered an amnesty and a ceasefire, the situation seems unlikely to be resolved in the foreseeable future. It is just one more of the endless conflicts to affect the troubled region of Southeast Asia.

Persistent rivalries

Because such conflicts are in many cases still going on, it is difficult to draw definitive conclusions about the history of Southeast Asia since 1945. However, a number of general points may be made. Although nationalism, in the form of the desire for independence from colonial rule, triumphed in the early stages of the postwar period, it is apparent that not all the countries of the region have been able to create a state acceptable to all the people living within it. In Burma, Thailand and the Philippines particularly, some groups would still like to form separate countries and have shown time and time again that they are prepared to fight for their cause, often using guerrilla techniques.

At the same time, pre-colonial rivalries have re-emerged, with all the traditional causes of conflict – racial, religious and territorial – being reasserted, most notably in the clashes between Vietnam and Kampuchea and between Vietnam and China since 1975. Even within ASEAN, which should be an alliance of friendly countries, rivalries persist. In this case the continued threat posed by Vietnamese operations in Kampuchea, the reality of superpower presence in the region and the possible results of further confrontation between China and the Soviet Union may help to create greater unity.

Even so, the communist victories in Indochina pose a threat to the independence of non-communist countries which may be too much for ASEAN alone to deal with, and for this reason the continued presence of the United States, with its naval base at Subic Bay in the Philippines, is clearly a crucial factor in maintaining stability at a strategic level, balancing the growing commitment of Soviet forces to the area and Chinese involvement in Indochina.

The continuing conflict

But this does little to prevent the high levels of conflict within the individual countries of Southeast Asia. There seems to be little hope of an end to the fighting in Kampuchea, for example, and Indonesia's war on East Timor, together with the various revolts in the Philippines, are likely to continue.

In addition, with leaders such as Lee Kuan Yew in Singapore and General Suharto in Indonesia now getting old, the potential for political chaos as they die or are replaced is apparent. This is particularly the case as the military coup has been an instrument of political change in many countries (notably Thailand, Burma and Indonesia) since the 1950s. Admittedly, some countries of the region – notably Singapore and Brunei – have found wealth and power, but their existence acts as a cruel comparison to the continuing poverty of others, both communist and non-communist. With population growth a major concern, the problems of Southeast Asia are by no means over.

Yet it is clear that, despite the incidence of conflict, Southeast Asia does have great potential for future development and wealth. Over half the world's population lives around the edges of the Pacific Ocean, across which more trade passes than across the Atlantic. Together with Japan, Taiwan and Hong Kong, Singapore has experienced tremendous economic growth in recent years, while the other members of ASEAN are numbered among 14 countries around the rim of the Pacific which have accounted for over half the world's economic growth in the years since 1980.

Indeed, it has been suggested that these countries around the Pacific, which include Southeast Asia, could play as important a role in global development in the 21st century as did the Mediterranean states in the 16th and the Atlantic states in the 18th, 19th and 20th centuries. It is an awesome prospect.

CONFLICT IN THE 20TH CENTURY: APPENDICES

Since the Second World War, the countries of Southeast Asia have been transformed by nationalist and communist movements from colonial territories to independent, if often unstable, nations. Personalities of widely varying background and style attended the birth of countries with equally distinct orientations. The region experienced fifteen major upheavals, the most devastating being the Vietnam War, which brought the full force of modern warfare to Indochina.

PERSONALITIES

Aung San (1915-1947) Burma's first postwar leader. After being active in student politics, he joined the "We Burmese" movement in 1938. In August 1940 he left Burma for Japan and headed the Burma Independence Army, formed by the Japanese in December 1941. Subsequently he headed the Anti-Fascist Organization (AFO) and Anti-Fascist People's Freedom League (AFPFL). Aung San changed sides in March 1945 and joined the Burma Executive Council in September 1946. He negotiated independence but was assassinated on July 19, 1947.

Chin Peng (1920-) Leader of the communist insurrection in postwar Malaya. Chin Peng was an officer in the Malayan Peoples' Anti-Japanese Army (MPAJA) during the Second World War and received the OBE for his services as chief liaison officer with the British Force 136. In March 1947 he became General Secretary of the Malayan Communist Party. He is said to be still at large.

Ngo Dinh Diem (1901-1963) President of South Vietnam. He entered the service of the Emperor, Bao Dai, and was Minister of Interior in Annam in 1933. Resigning after his reforms were rejected, he refused all offers from the Japanese, French and *Viet Minh* and went into voluntary exile in 1949. In June 1954, he became Prime Minister of South Vietnam under Bao Dai but

Ngo Dinh Diem

ousted the Emperor in the following year and became President of South Vietnam. He was deposed and murdered in a military coup on November 2, 1963.

Vo Nguyen Giap

Vo Nguyen Giap (1912-) Architect of North Vietnamese victory against both the French and the Americans. A history teacher, he joined the Indochinese Communist Party in the 1930s and fled to China in 1939. He helped organize the *Viet Minh* and was Minister of Interior in the Democratic Republic of Vietnam proclaimed in September 1945. Commander-in-Chief of the *Viet Minh* and the North Vietnamese Army, he was Deputy Prime Minister and Minister of Defense in the unified Vietnam, 1976-80, and a Politburo member until 1981.

Ho Chi Minh (1890-1969) North Vietnamese leader, he adopted the name Nguyen Ai Quoc (Nguyen the Patriot) and later that of Ho Chi Minh (He who enlightens). In 1911 he left Vietnam and went to Paris, Moscow, China, Thailand and Hong Kong, where he was imprisoned by the British authorities, 1931-32. He returned to organize the *Viet Minh* in Vietnam in May 1941 but was then briefly detained in China, 1942-43. He proclaimed the Democratic Republic of Vietnam in September 1945 and was President of North Vietnam from 1954 until his death.

Lee Kuan Yew (1923-) Singapore's first post-independence leader. He was a founder of the Socialist People's Action Party in 1954 and became a member of the Legislative Assembly in the following year. He became Prime Minister of Singapore in 1959, when the island became self-governing, and was then President of the Republic of Singapore upon independence in 1965, a post he still holds.

Ramon Magsaysay (1907-1957) Architect of the victory over the communist *Huks* in the Philippines. The general manager of a bus company before the Second World War, he became a guerrilla leader for the United States Forces in the Far East (USAFFE). After the liberation of the Philippines from the Japanese, he was military governor of West Luzon in 1945. Entering Congress in 1950, he was Secretary of Defense from September 1950 to February 1953. Joining the *Nacionalistas*, he won the presidential election in November 1953 and remained President of the Philippines until he died in an air crash in March 1957.

Ferdinand Edralin Marcos (1917-) President of the Philippines. During the Second World War he served as a captain in the USAFFE. A special assistant to President Roxas, 1946-47, he was elected to the House of Representatives in 1949 and became a member of the Senate in 1959. Leader of the Senate from 1963, he became President of the Philippines in 1965. Marcos also occupied the office of prime minister from 1973. He was finally eased from power in February 1986.

Pol Pot (1928-) Leader of the Khmer Rouge. He was born Saloth Sar and as well as being known as Pol Pot, he has been called Tol Saut. A shadowy figure, he was briefly a novice in a monastery and spent the years from 1949 to 1953 in France studying technical education. Returning to Cambodia in 1953, he had become General Secretary of the Khmer Rouge by 1962. He was Prime Minister of Kampuchea from 1976 until the Vietnamese invasion in 1979. He was displaced as leader of the Khmer Rouge in 1979 but is still believed to be active in the movement.

Prince Norodom Sihanouk (1922-) King of Cambodia. Son of King Norodom Suramarit, he was elected King himself in April 1941 but abdicated in March 1955. He then served as Prime Minister of Cambodia from 1955 to 1960 and as Head of State from 1960 until ousted in a coup in March 1970. Allied with the Khmer Rouge, he was restored as Head of State in April 1975 but was forced out in April 1976. Head of the *Moulinaka* movement since 1981, he is also leader of the Coalition Government of Democratic Kampuchea, the government in exile formed in 1983.

T N J Suharto (1921-) President of Indonesia. An officer in the Japanese-sponsored Indonesian Army, he became a regimental commander in 1945. He became Deputy Chief of Staff from 1960 to 1965 and Chief of Staff from 1965 to 1968. Following a failed communist coup, he and a group of army officers deposed Sukarno in 1967. Suharto was acting President from 1967 to 1968, Supreme Commander from 1968 to 1973 and has been President of Indonesia from March 1968 onward.

Kusno Sosro Sukarno (1901-1970) Indonesia's first President. He became involved in nationalist politics in 1927 and was detained by the Dutch authorities from 1929-32. He was then exiled to a remote island but was released by the Japanese in 1942. He became President of the Republic of Indonesia, proclaimed in 1945, and President of the United States of Indonesia upon full independence in 1949. He was also Prime Minister (1959-66) and Head of State (1963-66), while retaining the presidency until 1967, when all power devolved upon the army. He was kept under house arrest until his death.

Nguyen Van Thieu (1923-) President of South Vietnam. He served in the French-sponsored Vietnamese Nationalist Army from 1948-54. He then served in the South Vietnamese Army, commanding the 1st Infantry Division (1960-62), the 5th Infantry Division (1962-63) and the IV Corps (1963-64). He became Deputy Prime Minister and Minister of Defense in 1964 and subsequently Head of State. In 1967 he became President and remained so until 1975.

Ferdinand Marcos

Prince Norodom Sihanouk

Kusno Sukarno

POLITICAL UPDATE

Burma
Capital: Rangoon
Population: 39.6 million
Constitution: Socialist Republic following the "Burmese Way to Socialism"
Orientation: Has friendship and nonaggression treaty with the People's Republic of China (1960)
Armed Forces: Army 170,000; Navy 7,000; Air Force 9,000
Opponents: Over 38,000 guerrillas including the Burmese Communist Party (20,000), the Kachin Independence Army (5,000), the Shan United Army (4,000) the Karen National Liberation Army (4,000) and the Shan State Army (3,500)

Brunei
Capital: Bandar Seri Begawan
Population: 240,000
Constitution: Absolute monarchy until independence in 1984 but now with ministerial system of government
Orientation: Defense agreement with Britain, which stations some Gurkhas there. Joined ASEAN in 1984
Armed Forces: Army 3,400; Navy 450; Air Force 200
Opponents: The Parti Rakyat Brunei, responsible for the 1962 revolt, still exists

Indonesia
Capital: Jakarta
Population: 161 million
Constitution: Republic but with strong military presence and leadership since 1965
Orientation: Member of ASEAN and of the Non-Aligned Movement. Receives some military assistance from the United States and from Australia
Armed Forces: Army 216,000; Navy 36,950; Air Force 25,100
Opponents: Fretilin (700) on East Timor and the Free Papua Movement (100)

Kampuchea
Capital: Phnom Penh
Population: 6 million
Constitution: Socialist Republic under Vietnamese military occupation
Orientation: Friendship treaties with Bulgaria (1960) and East Germany (1980) and agreements on military provisions with Vietnam (1979 and 1982)
Armed Forces: Army 35,000
Opponents: The forces of the Coalition Government of Democratic Kampuchea embracing the Khmer Rouge, *Moulinaka* and the Khmer People's National Liberation Front (together perhaps over 60,000)

Laos
Capital: Vientiane
Population: 3.7 million
Constitution: Socialist Republic
Orientation: Friendship treaties with Bulgaria (1979), Czechoslovakia (1980) and military agreements with

Indonesian Army shows its strength after downfall of Sukarno.

Vietnam (1977)
Armed Forces: Army 50,000; Navy 1,700; Air Force 2,000

Malaysia
Capital: Kuala Lumpur
Population: 16.3 million
Constitution: Federation
Orientation: Member of ASEAN. Defense agreement known as the Five-Power Defense Arrangements (Australia, Britain, Malaysia, New Zealand and Singapore) of 1971 still exists. Britain withdrew forces in 1976 but Australian forces remain.
Armed Forces: Army 90,000; Navy 9,000; Air Force 11,000
Opponents: Malayan Communist Party (1,000) and Marxist/Leninist faction of the Malayan Communist Party (450)

Philippines
Capital: Manila
Population: 55 million
Constitution: Republic
Orientation: Member of ASEAN. Mutual Cooperation and Security Treaty with the United States (1951 and 1983) with major US base facilities (renewed 1983)
Armed Forces: Army 70,000; Navy 28,000; Air Force 16,800
Opponents: Moro National Liberation Army on Mindanao (1,000) and Maoist New People's Army on Luzon and other islands (11,000)

Singapore
Population: 2.6 million
Constitution: Republic dominated by People's Action Party
Orientation: Member of ASEAN. Signatory to Five-Power Agreement in 1971 and has Australian and New Zealand forces stationed on the island. Has training school in Brunei
Armed Forces: Army 45,000; Navy 4,500; Air Force 6,000

Thailand
Capital: Bangkok
Population: 51.7 million
Constitution: Constitutional monarchy since 1932 but has had a succession of military governments, the last civilian government being overthrown in 1976. In fact, there were 14 coups or attempted coups between 1933 and 1981.
Orientation: Member of ASEAN. Receives military assistance from the United States under the Manila Pact of 1954 (the last vestige of SEATO) and from Australia
Armed Forces: Army 160,000; Navy 32,200; Marines 13,000; Air Force 43,100
Opponents: Malayan Communist Party (1,500) and Thai Communist Party (500); Thai People's Revolutionary Movement (250). Also threats of Vietnamese advances from Kampuchea and occasional opposition from hill tribes

Vietnam
Capital: Hanoi
Population: 60 million
Constitution: Socialist Republic
Orientation: Treaty of Friendship, Cooperation and Mutual Assistance with the Soviet Union (1978); friendship treaties with Bulgaria (1979), Cuba (1982), Czechoslovakia (1980) and East Germany (1977). Military agreements with Laos (1977) and Kampuchea (1979 and 1982).
Armed Forces: Army 1 million; Navy 12,000; Air Force 15,000. Of the armed forces, 40,000 are in Laos and 160,000 in Kampuchea
Opponents: see Kampuchea. Also the People's Republic of China

The army celebrates the Philippines' tenth independence day, 1956.

36946

SUMMARY OF CONFLICTS

The Indonesian War for Independence, 1945-49

Indonesian nationalists proclaimed independence on August 17, 1945, and fighting broke out when British forces reoccupied Java in September. During 1946 the Dutch resumed responsibility and undertook some negotiations. However, the Dutch remained committed to regaining control by military means and launched major offensives in June 1947 and December 1948. Indonesian guerrilla tactics and international pressure forced the Dutch to give up sovereignty on November 2, 1949. The Dutch retained control of West Irian until 1962.

First Indochina War, 1945-54

Following the Japanese collapse, *Viet Minh* forces seized control of much of Vietnam. However, the French were determined to regain power and fighting began when British forces arrived to restore order in September 1945. Following abortive negotiations, fighting broke out between the French and the *Viet Minh* in November 1946. French forces withdrew to the Red River and Mekong deltas in 1949 and held off *Viet Minh* assaults but attempts to carry the war back into *Viet Minh* territory were generally unsuccessful. The last such attempt resulted in the disastrous battle at Dien Bien Phu in 1954. A peace conference at Geneva concluded on July 21 with agreements giving independence to Laos, Cambodia and Vietnam, which was split between a communist north and a Western-oriented south.

The Huk Rebellion in the Philippines, 1946-54

A communist-controlled peasant uprising began in the summer of 1946 in the central provinces of Luzon. The communist guerrillas or *Huks* were initially successful until the appointment of Ramon Magsaysay as Secretary for National Defense in September 1950. Magsaysay reorganized the armed forces and undertook a coordinated hearts and minds campaign that led to the end of the *Huk* uprising by 1954 although some pockets of resistance remained.

The Malayan Emergency, 1948-60

A communist uprising began in June 1948, the Malayan Races Liberation Army (MRLA) being the military front of the Malayan Communist Party (MCP). The rebels had some success but were dependent for support upon the minority Chinese population and "squatters" living along the jungle edges. A sophisticated British campaign started by Sir Harold Briggs undermined support for the guerrillas. In any case the British had already declared an interest in early independence and the Malayan government was able to declare the emergency at an end in July 1960. Some guerrillas remain in the remote jungle areas close to the Thai-Malay frontier.

The Karen Revolt in Burma, 1949-55

One of a number of uprisings which plagued the newly independent state of Burma, the Karens wanted their own state. The Karen National Defense Organization (KNDO) responded to government massacres of Karen tribesmen by seizing a number of towns in January 1949. The rebels failed to take Rangoon and were forced into guerrilla warfare. Most fighting had subsided by 1955.

The Second Indochina War or Vietnam War, 1957-75

North Vietnam never accepted the Geneva agreements of 1954 and began to infiltrate guerrillas into South Vietnam from 1957 onwards. In 1960 the National Liberation

British police officer and Gurkhas raid communist hideout, Malaya 1948.

Front (NLF) or Viet Cong were recognized. United States assistance steadily increased as the South Vietnamese government came under heavy pressure in the countryside of South Vietnam. The US bombing of North Vietnam began in February 1965, after the United States had decided on a larger commitment following the Gulf of Tonkin incident in August 1964. Ground forces arrived in March 1965 and US strength continued to increase.

However, US forces, those of allied states and the South Vietnamese Army (ARVN) were unable to defeat the Viet Cong and its North Vietnamese regular allies (NVA). Opposition to the war grew in the United States and, after the shock of the Tet offensive, President Nixon was elected in 1968 to find a solution. A policy of "Vietnamization" saw the progressive reduction of US forces although Nixon was prepared to widen the war in order to put additional pressure on the North Vietnamese negotiators at the talks in Paris which had begun in January 1969. Ultimately the unbridled use of US air power brought a ceasefire agreement in January 1973 and US forces pulled out. However, large areas of South Vietnam remained in communist hands and in March 1975 the NVA offensive led to a rapid collapse of the south. Saigon fell in April 1975.

The War in Laos, 1958-75

French withdrawal in 1954 left Laos effectively divided between the two royal half-brothers, Prince Souvana Phouma and Prince Souphanouvong. The former controlled the Royal Laotian forces and the latter the communist Pathet Lao. Fighting broke out in 1958 although it was ended by a temporary truce in July 1962. Fighting began again in 1963 with the United States giving assistance to the Royal Laotian forces and the North Vietnamese aiding the Pathet Lao. While US bombing in North Vietnam ceased between 1968 and 1972, that in Laos continued and the ARVN and US forces crossed into Laos to close the Ho Chi Minh Trail in February 1971. A ceasefire was agreed in February 1973 but, as in South Vietnam, a communist offensive in early 1975 saw the fall of the capital, Vientiane, in June and the proclamation of a communist republic under Prince Souphanouvong in December 1975.

The War in Cambodia, 1963-75

After French withdrawal, the government of Prince Sihanouk faced a small-scale uprising waged by the communist Khmer Rouge, which increased after 1963. Sihanouk was successful in containing the uprising and maintaining Cambodia's neutrality although Cambodian territory was used by Viet Cong and NVA units infiltrating South Vietnam along the Ho Chi Minh Trail. However, Sihanouk was overthrown by Lon Nol in March 1970 and joined the Khmer Rouge. His appeal for support greatly assisted the cause of the Khmer Rouge. Lon Nol received US assistance and in April 1970 US and ARVN forces were committed to Cambodia. However, this action caused major disruption in Cambodia, which brought the Khmer Rouge support. Although North Vietnamese pressure was reduced after the ceasefire in South Vietnam in 1973, the Khmer Rouge continued to score successes and Phnom Penh fell in April 1975.

The Malaysian Confrontation, 1963-66

Indonesia strongly opposed the creation of a Malaysian federation embracing the territories of Sarawak, Brunei and North Borneo (Sabah) and, in December 1962, backed a revolt against the Sultan of Brunei. As the revolt subsided, Indonesian "volunteers" were sent to Sarawak in April 1963. Following the formation of Malaysia in September 1963 Indonesian regular troops were committed. An extension of the successful British techniques perfected in Malaya resulted in few successes for the Indonesians and the popularity of Sukarno, Indonesia's president, dwindled. Following an attempted communist coup in September 1965, the Indonesian army took over power. The army began negotiations which resulted in an end to confrontation in August 1966.

New People's Army insurgency in the Philippines, 1969-

The military wing of the Maoist Communist Party of the Philippines, Marxist-Leninist, known as the New People's Army (NPA), began fighting in March 1969 in the old *Huk* province of Tarlac on Luzon. The strength of the NPA has steadily increased and, by 1985, it was in a strong position even in the southern island of Mindanao.

Moro insurgency on Mindanao in the Philippines, 1972-

Inheritors of a strong anti-central tradition, the Muslim Moros began fighting for separation from the Philippines in September 1972. The military wing of the Moro National Liberation Front (MNLF) is the *Bangsa Moro* Army.

Vietnamese invasion and occupation of Kampuchea, 1978-79

Relations between Vietnam and the Khmer Rouge government of Kampuchea (formerly Cambodia) deteriorated after the communist victories of 1975. Increasing border incidents resulted in a full-scale Vietnamese invasion in December 1978, Phnom Penh falling in January 1979.

Insurgency in Kampuchea, 1979-

Following the Vietnamese occupation of Kampuchea, a number of groups have resisted the continuing Vietnamese presence. The largest forces opposed to the Vietnamese are the Khmer Rouge but there are also Son Sann's Khmer People's National Liberation Front (KPNLF) and Prince Sihanouk's *Moulinaka* movement. The three groups formed a coalition under Sihanouk's leadership in June 1983. Vietnamese occupation of Kampuchea is not recognized by the United Nations.

Laotian communist forces training in 1972.

LAND WARFARE VIETNAM

When American soldiers were first deployed to Vietnam in 1965, they were not prepared for the sort of war that was being fought. Ready for large-scale battles, in which numbers, firepower and technology were the keys to victory, they encountered soldiers of the North Vietnamese Army (NVA) and Viet Cong (VC) who preferred to fight unconventional wars using guerrilla-style ambushes or hit-and-run raids in inhospitable terrain.

The aim of American strategy was therefore to force the enemy into an open battle which he could not hope to win, and this was carried out in two principal ways. In what were known as "fix and destroy" missions, American air or ground surveillance teams would locate enemy concentrations and then call in superior forces to destroy them.

As such forces needed to move quickly, the helicopter became increasingly important, particularly in the hands of units such as the 1st Cavalry Division (Airmobile). As soon as a location had been chosen, reconnaissance helicopters would select a landing zone (LZ) and, as attack helicopters such as UH-1 or AH-1 gunships laid down

AH-1G Huey Cobra

AH-1G Huey Cobra
The principal helicopter gunship in US service by the late 1960s, armed with machine guns and rockets for hitting ground targets around an LZ.

CH-47C Chinook
Used to carry troops (up to 44), supplies and even underslung loads such as artillery pieces into a prepared LZ or firebase.

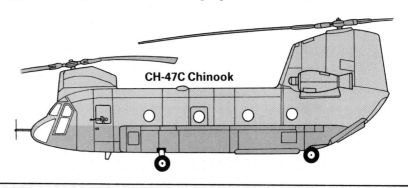

CH-47C Chinook

suppressive fire, special teams would be landed to clear the site. They would be followed by units of infantry, carried aboard UH-1D or CH-47 Chinook helicopters and, as they established a ground position, other helicopters would provide fire support, even bringing in artillery pieces if needed.

But such a position was only meant to be temporary, acting as a base from which to destroy precise enemy forces. An alternative was to set up more permanent firebases

(see below) which, positioned astride infiltration routes, would act as a focus for NVA/VC attack. Once that developed, fire from 105mm field guns, mortars and aircraft would destroy the enemy units. By 1968 the Americans had established whole networks of mutually supporting firebases which were enjoying some success. In the end, however, the enemy bypassed American bases, concentrating on controlling villages.

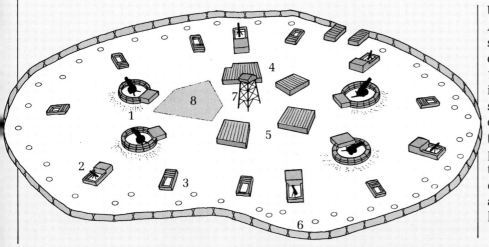

US Firebase
A firebase was designed to be a self-contained defensive location, comprising emplacements for 105mm artillery (1), mortars (2) and infantry troops (3). These would be situated around a command complex (4) and fire control posts (5), and surrounded by a mined perimeter fence (6). An observation tower (7) would enable the defenders to see over a wide area and a helicopter LZ (8) acted as the link with the outside.

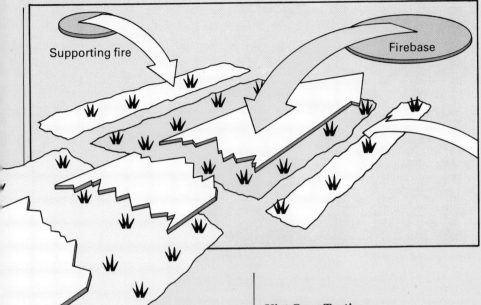

Firebase Defense

NVA/VC line of advance

Artillery "box:" artillery from a firebase fires on NVA/VC attackers

Attackers hedged in by fire from support firebases

Air support from USAF B-52s, which concentrate on bombing rear and reserves

NVA/VC advance column is broken up by the sheer weight of US firepower

Firebase Defense

If the main aim of the firebase was to act as an anvil against which NVA or VC attacks could be broken, defense was clearly essential. Usually, firebases were situated so that they could be mutually supporting, with artillery fire from one base contributing to the defense of its neighbors. If an enemy attack materialized (as above), such artillery fire could be laid along the line of advance, breaking the attack up and destroying its momentum. At the same time, airpower could also be deployed, including the awesome B-52s. The effects could be devastating, proving for all to see that US firepower was formidable. Unfortunately, it was not enough.

Viet Cong Tactics

The VC were essentially revolutionary guerrillas. They knew they were weak in the face of massive American firepower and airpower, but they did enjoy certain strengths which the Americans proved unable to undermine. Chief among these was "popular" support, for VC activists always "melted away" when pursued, disappearing into elaborate tunnel complexes (as below) or blending into everyday life.

The "safe bases" in the villages of the South often had to be defended, particularly when the Americans sent in patrols intent on "fix and destroy" missions. As the VC lacked the conventional advantages of state-sponsored forces – military cohesion, the latest weapons and

technology, firepower and air strength – they inevitably engaged in guerrilla warfare.

Thus, when an American patrol entered a given area, messages would be transmitted to some form of central command and orders given for guerrilla attacks. Tunnels with many exits enabled VC fighters to appear unexpectedly, ambushing and sniping the enemy. American troops had no idea where the attacks came from and, when gradually demoralized by VC traps – special pits lined with sharpened bamboo punji stakes, mines and grenade booby-traps – would probably respond with violence against innocent villagers. This forced many villagers into the arms of the VC. Once that happened, the Americans had lost.

Viet Cong Tunnel System

1 Hut concealing entrance shaft
2 Guardroom
3 Hospital area
4 Concealed shafts – for access and/or ventilation
5 Underwater entrance
6 Surface observation post
7 Stores
8 Armory

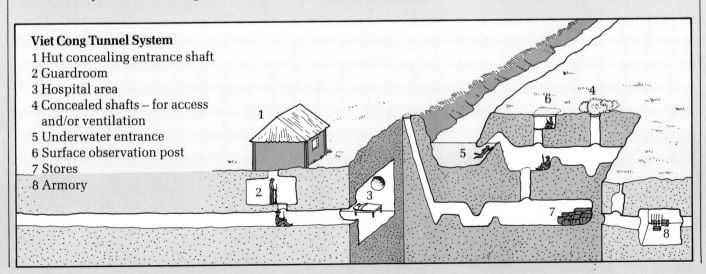

AIR WARFARE VIETNAM

Linebacker I

Throughout the Vietnam War, Viet Cong guerrillas and North Vietnamese regulars entered the South by means of jungle tracks which were difficult to block on the ground. The Ho Chi Minh Trail, for example, constantly changed its route, while the DMZ (demilitarized zone) was not supposed to contain US troops.

An answer to this problem was provided by airpower and new electronic devices. Special monitoring devices known as ADSIDs (air delivered seismic intruder devices) were dropped into likely infiltration areas.

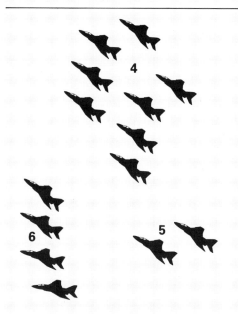

One advantage that the Americans enjoyed over their enemies in Vietnam was access to virtually unlimited airpower. This was used to carry out three basic roles: reconnaissance, strike and surveillance.

Reconnaissance missions, flown by camera-equipped aircraft such as the RF-4 Phantom, provided photographic evidence of enemy bases, infiltration routes and supply dumps. Such information enabled strike aircraft carrying high-explosive bombs, missiles and (in 1972) laser-guided "smart" bombs, to carry out attacks, protected by specialized aircraft designed to jam enemy radars or seek out and destroy antiaircraft defenses.

Tactical aircraft such as F-100s or F-4s were normally used for strike missions, but the Americans occasionally used B-52 strategic bombers.

Finally, aircraft could be used to monitor enemy infiltration routes, using seismic devices and other electronic aids, relaying the information to strike formations. By the 1970s, RPVs (remotely-piloted vehicles) carried out this role.

North Vietnamese Air Defense

The North Vietnamese made great efforts to defend themselves against the American bombing raids. Against low-flying aircraft, they used machine guns such as the Chinese 7.92mm Type 24, but it was the high-flying aircraft which did most damage. Soviet-supplied anti-aircraft guns such as the 37mm M38/39 were quite effective, although the real worry to the Americans were the SAMs. Radar-controlled missiles such as the SA-2 would suddenly appear, homing in on the heat of the aircraft exhausts. The North Vietnamese used Soviet MiG fighters, but ineffectively.

North Vietnamese antiaircraft battery

If human beings came near, these sent out a signal to a circling aircraft such as a Beech A-36 Bonanza, which would then relay it to a high-flying control aircraft such as a Lockheed EC-121R. From there, it would go to a ground-based Infiltration Surveillance Center which would assess it and, if found to be useful, use it as a basis for strike missions. Because of pilot losses, by the early 1970s the Americans had substituted RPVs such as the Ryan Model 147SC for the monitoring aircraft and had even experimented with RPVs fitted with their own strike missiles for immediate response.

F-4 Phantom II fighters drop their bomb loads over North Vietnam, 1972.

Bombing the North

Between March 1965 and November 1968, the Americans used their airpower to bomb targets in North Vietnam: an operation known as Rolling Thunder. It was not particularly effective: the aircraft were deliberately kept away from built-up areas and the bombs in use were not very accurate.

The bombing did not resume until 1972 when, in response to the North Vietnamese invasion of the South, President Nixon authorized a series of raids known as Linebacker I, in which the new "smart" bombs were used to devastating effect. In December, Linebacker II was initiated, in which B-52s were allowed to hit Hanoi and Haiphong for an 11-day period. The North Vietnamese responded by beginning serious peace talks. Any raid into the North had to be protected, and by 1972 an elaborate "package" of integrated airpower had been developed, as shown below. A typical Linebacker I raid would begin with "Iron Hand" strikes (1), in which F-4 and F-105 aircraft would seek out and destroy enemy SAM or antiaircraft gun sites, clearing the way for the main force. This would be spearheaded by A-7 Corsair IIs (2), dispensing radar-disrupting "chaff" and protected by combat air patrol F-4s (3). The Strike group (4) of F-4s, armed with ordinary and smart bombs, would then arrive, protected by close-support (5) and free-roaming (6) fighters. Finally, reconnaissance RF-4s (7) would take photographs of the damage.

CHRONOLOGY

1941

December 7 Japanese attack on Pearl Harbor

1942

February 15 Surrender of Singapore to the Japanese

February 27 Battle of the Java Sea

March 9 Surrender of Dutch East Indies to the Japanese

March 29 Formation of *Hukbalahap* in the Philippines

May 6 Surrender of Corregidor to the Japanese

May 7-8 Battle of the Coral Sea

June 4 Battle of Midway

1943

August 1 Burma granted "independence" by Japan

1945

March 9 Japanese coup in French Indochina

March 11 French Indochina granted "independence" by Japan

August 15 Japanese announce surrender

August 17 Indonesian nationalists proclaim independence of the Dutch East Indies

September 2 Official surrender of Japan to the Allies; Ho Chi Minh proclaims independence of a Democratic Republic of Vietnam in Hanoi

September 11 British forces occupy Saigon

September 29 British forces occupy Java

1946

January 7 France gives limited autonomy to Cambodia

March 16 French forces occupy Hanoi

May 15 British forces leave Indochina

July 4 The Philippines become independent from the United States

August 27 France gives limited autonomy to Laos

November 5 Linggadjati agreement between the Dutch and Indonesian nationalists

1947

June 20 First Dutch "police action" in Indonesia

1948

January 4 Burma becomes independent from Britain

June 17 Declaration of a state of emergency in Malaya

December 18 Second Dutch "police action" in Indonesia

1949

July 19 France recognizes sovereignty of Laos

October 1 Proclamation of the Chinese People's Republic

November 2 Indonesia given its sovereignty by the Dutch

November 8 France recognizes sovereignty of Cambodia

December 27 Indonesian sovereignty comes into effect

1950

August 17 Indonesia becomes a republic

1953

October 22 France grants full independence to Laos

November 9 France grants full independence to Cambodia

November 20 French forces occupy Dien Bien Phu

1954

May 8 Final surrender of French forces at Dien Bien Phu

May 8 International conference begins at Geneva

July 21 Geneva agreements recognize independence for Laos and Cambodia, and give independence to North Vietnam and South Vietnam from France

September 8 Creation of the Southeast Asia Treaty Organization (SEATO) at Manila

1955

April 18-24 Conference of 29 non-aligned states at Bandung in Indonesia

1957

August 31 Malaya becomes independent from Britain

1959

May 30 Lee Kuan Yew becomes Prime Minister of Singapore

July 8 First American casualty in South Vietnam

1960

July 31 End of the state of emergency in Malaya

1962

December 8 Brunei revolt

1963

April 12 Start of Malaysian "Confrontation" with Indonesia

August 31 Singapore becomes independent from Britain

September 16 Formation of Federation of Malaysia

1964

August 2 Gulf of Tonkin incident

August 7 US Congress passes Gulf of Tonkin Resolution

August 17 Attempted Indonesian landings in Malaya

1965

February 7 US bombing of North Vietnam begins

March 8 Arrival of first US ground forces in South Vietnam

August 9 Singapore leaves the Malaysian Federation

September 30 Attempted communist coup in Indonesia

1966

March 12 Suharto takes power in Indonesia

August 11 End of Malaysian "Confrontation"

1967

September 3 General Van Thieu becomes President of South Vietnam

1968

January 21 North Vietnamese start siege of Khe Sanh at beginning of their Tet offensive

April 14 Siege of Khe Sanh lifted

October 31 US pause in bombing of North Vietnam

1969

January 25 Peace talks on Vietnam open in Paris

1970

March 18 Lon Nol ousts Sihanouk from power in Cambodia

June 24 US Congress repeals Gulf of Tonkin Resolution

1972

April 2 US resumes bombing of North Vietnam

September 23 Declaration of martial law in the Philippines

October 23 US pause in bombing of North Vietnam

December 19-30 US Linebacker II bombing campaign

1973

January 9 Agreement on ceasefire in South Vietnam reached at Paris

January 27 Ceasefire comes into effect in South Vietnam

March 29 Last US forces leave South Vietnam

1975

April 17 Fall of Phnom Penh to Khmer Rouge

April 30 Fall of Saigon to North Vietnamese

November 28 Fretilin declares independence in East Timor

December 3 Proclamation of People's Democratic Republic of Laos

December 7 Indonesian invasion of East Timor

1976

June 30 Closure of SEATO headquarters in Bangkok

1977

October 10 Moros kill 36 army officers in Philippines

1978

November 3 Treaty between Vietnam and the Soviet Union

December 25 Vietnam invades Kampuchea

1979

January 7 Fall of Phnom Penh to Vietnamese

February 17 Chinese People's Republic invades Vietnam

March 16 Withdrawal of Chinese forces from Vietnam

1983

August 21 Murder of Philippines Opposition leader, Benigno Aquino

1984

January 1 Full independence of Brunei

1985

November 3 Announcement of Philippines' presidential election

December 3 Announcement of presidential candidacy of Mrs. Aquino in Philippines

1986

February 7 Presidential elections in Philippines

February 25 President Marcos flees Philippines

INDEX

FURTHER READING

Andaya, B. W. and L. Y., *A History of Malaysia* (St. Martin's, New York, 1984)

Clutterbuck, R., *Conflict and Violence in Singapore and Malaysia, 1945-1983* (Westview, Boulder, CO, 1984)

Crouch, H., *The Army and Politics in Indonesia* (Cornell Univ. Pr., Ithaca, NY, 1978)

Dommen, A. J., *Laos: The Keystone of Indochina* (Westview, Boulder, CO, 1985)

Dunn, P., *The First Vietnam War* (St. Martin's, New York, 1985)

Fall, B., *Hell in a Very Small Place: The Siege of Dien Bien Phu* (DaCapo, New York, 1985)

Irving, R. E. M., *The First Indochina War: French and American Policy, 1945 to 1954* (Books on Demand, Ann Arbor, MI, 1975)

James, H. and Shiel-Small, D., *The Undeclared War: The Story of the Indonesian Confrontation, 1962-1966* (Rowman & Littlefield, Totowa, NJ, 1971)

Karnow, S., *Vietnam: A History* (Penguin, New York, 1984)

Kiernam, B., *How Pol Pot Came to Power* (Schocken, New York, 1985)

Lawson, D., *The New Philippines* (Watts, New York, 1986)

Lewy, G., *America in Vietnam* (Oxford Univ. Pr., New York, 1978)

Mackie, J. A. C., *Konfrontasi: The Indonesia-Malaya Dispute, 1963-1966* (Oxford Univ. Pr., New York, 1974)

Maclear, M., *The Ten Thousand Day War: Vietnam, 1945-1975* (Avon Bks., New York, 1982)

Osborne, M., *Southeast Asia*, 3rd ed. (Allen and Unwin, Winchester, MA, 1985)

Palmer, D., *Summons of the Trumpet: US-Vietnam in Perspective* (Presidio, Novato, CA, 1978)

Ranjit Singh, D. S., *Brunei, 1839-1983: The Problems of Political Survival* (Oxford Univ. Pr., New York, 1984)

Ricklefs, M. C., *A History of Modern Indonesia* (Indiana Univ. Pr., Bloomington, IN, 1981)

Samudavanija, C-A., *The Thai Young Turks* (Gower Pub. Co., Brookfield, VT, 1982)

Shawcross, W., *The Quality of Mercy: Cambodia, Holocaust and Modern Conscience* (Simon & Schuster, New York, 1984)

Short, A., *The Communist Insurrection in Malaya, 1948-60* (Crane Russak, New York, 1974)

Steinberg, D. I., *Burma: A Socialist Nation* (Westview, Boulder, CO, 1982)

ACKNOWLEDGMENTS

Cover: Popperfoto; contents page: Robert Hunt; page 7: Hutchinson; page 8: Topham; page 9: Hutchinson; page 10: Photosource/Keystone; page 12: Robert Hunt; page 15: Popperfoto; page 17 (left): Photosource/Keystone; page 17 (right): MARS; page 19: Robert Hunt; page 20: Colorific; page 21: Photosource; pages 22-23: Photosource/Keystone; page 24: The Research House/TA Davis; page 25: Photosource/Keystone; page 26: Topham; page 29: Photosource/Three Lions; page 30: MARS; page 31 (both): MARS; page 32: Photosource/Central Press; page 33: MARS; page 34: Photosource/Central Press; page 35 (both): MARS; pages 36-37: Rex Features; page 37: Photosource; page 38: Network/Mike Goldwater; page 39: Popperfoto; page 40 (both): Photosource; page 42: Photosource/Keystone; page 44: Frank Spooner; page 45: Topham; page 46: Photosource; page 48 (top): Popperfoto; page 48 (bottom): Camera Press; page 49 (left): Camera Press; page 49 (center): Popperfoto; page 49 (right): Popperfoto; page 50: Photosource/Keystone; page 51: Photosource/Keystone; page 5: Colorific; page 53: Photosource/Keystone; page 57: The Research House.